THE MIDDLE SCHOOL
PRINCIPAL'S
CALENDAR

To our families—for their love and support
To our students—our hope for the future
To our colleagues—who gave us the gift of their professional practices

THE MIDDLE SCHOOL
PRINCIPAL'S CALENDAR

A MONTH-BY-MONTH PLANNER
FOR THE SCHOOL YEAR

ROBERT RICKEN • MICHAEL TERC

CORWIN PRESS, INC.
A Sage Publications Company
Thousand Oaks, California

For information:

 Corwin Press, Inc.
A Sage Publications Company
2455 Teller Road
Thousand Oaks, California 91320
www.corwinpress.com

Sage Publications Ltd.
6 Bonhill Street
London EC2A 4PU
United Kingdom

Sage Publications India Pvt. Ltd.
B-42, Panchsheel Enclave
Post Box 4109
New Delhi 110 017 India

Printed in the United States of America

Library of Congress Cataloging-in-Publication Data

Ricken, Robert.
The middle school principal's calendar: A month-by-month planner for the
school year / Robert Ricken, Michael Terc.
    p. cm.
ISBN 0–7619–3978–4 (Cloth)—ISBN 0–7619–3979–2 (Paper)
    1. Schedules, School—United States—Handbooks, manuals, etc. 2. Middle school
principals—United States-Handbooks, manuals, etc. I. Terc, Michael. II. Title.
LB3032.R56 2004
373.12´42—dc21

                                           2003008481

03   04   05   06   10   9   8   7   6   5   4   3   2   1

Acquisitions Editor:	Robert D. Clouse
Associate Editor:	Kristen Gibson
Editorial Assistant:	Jingle Vea
Production Editor:	Melanie Birdsall
Copy Editor:	Cheryl Duksta
Typesetter:	C&M Digitals (P) Ltd.
Proofreader:	Cheryl Rivard
Cover Designer:	Tracy E. Miller
Production Artist:	Lisa Miller

Contents

Resources

Preface

We sincerely believe that the only positive example of restructuring American education in the past half century was the movement that developed the middle school to replace the traditional junior high school. Collectively, we have completed more than seventy years as educators, but our time spent in the middle school remains our most rewarding career experience. The ideas of our dynamic staff constantly raised the expectations we had for our students. Their collaborative planning enabled us to both anticipate problems and assertively solve long-standing issues that had stymied our predecessors. Middle-level children discovered an oasis of sanity in our school as they attempted to address the problems of our society and the trials of preadolescence.

Our calendar is intended to serve as a living document. Every entry we've made is incomplete since it lacks your interpretation and the expertise you bring to your position. It is our intent to stimulate the thinking, planning, and implementation phases of a staff's attempt to restructure its educational environment. Our description of many ideas that have proven to be successful in other middle schools may not always be suitable for your building. Use those you find relevant, but feel free to discard items that do not meet your present needs. We placed blank spaces after each activity description in the hopes that you will provide your input and thereby become our coauthors.

A more thorough definition of leadership is necessary since middle school principals must develop staff members who believe they can contribute to every aspect of the school's program and tone. It takes a multitalented professional who is not intimidated by teacher involvement in the decision-making process to run a middle-level school. Having the following qualities and using the organizational skills in our text will help the middle school administrator to truly become a leader of leaders.

Recently a New York State Education Department Blue Ribbon Panel on School Leadership developed a list of essential knowledge and skills of effective school leaders. We believe these nine characteristics serve as a model for middle school administrators.

Essential Knowledge and Skills for Effective School Leadership Characteristics

1. Leaders know and understand what it means and what it takes to be a leader.

Leadership is the act of identifying important goals and then motivating and enabling others to devote themselves and all necessary resources to achievement. It includes summoning one's self and others to learn and adapt to the new situation represented by the goal.

2. Leaders have a vision for schools that they constantly share and promote.

Leaders have a vision of the ideal and can articulate this vision to any audience and work diligently to make it a reality. Leaders also know how to build upon and sustain a vision that preceded them.

3. Leaders communicate clearly and effectively.

Leaders possess effective writing and presentation skills. They express themselves clearly and are confident and capable of responding to the hard questions in a public forum. They are also direct and precise questioners, always seeking understanding.

4. Leaders collaborate and cooperate with others.

Leaders communicate high expectations and provide accurate information to foster understanding and to maintain trust and confidence. Leaders reach out to others for support and assistance, build partnerships, secure resources, and share credit for successes and accomplishments. School leaders manage change through effective relationships with school boards.

5. Leaders persevere and take the "long view."

Leaders build institutions that endure. They "stay the course," maintain focus, and anticipate and work to overcome resistance. They create capacity within the organization to achieve and sustain its vision.

6. Leaders support, develop, and nurture staff.

Leaders set a standard for ethical behavior. They seek diverse perspectives and alternative points of view. They encourage initiative, innovation, collaboration, and a strong work ethic. Leaders expect and provide opportunities for staff to engage in continuous personal and professional growth. They recognize individual talents and assign responsibility and authority for specific tasks. Leaders celebrate accomplishments. They identify, recruit, mentor, and promote potential leaders.

7. Leaders hold themselves and others responsible and accountable.

Leaders embrace and adhere to comprehensive planning that improves the organization. They use data to determine the present state of the organization, identify root-cause problems, propose solutions, and validate accomplishments. Leaders respect responsibility and accountability and manage resources effectively and efficiently. They require staff to establish and meet clear indicators of success. Leaders in education also know and understand good pedagogy and effective classroom practices and support sustained professional development. They recognize the importance of learning standards and significance of assessments.

8. Leaders never stop learning and honing their skills.

Leaders are introspective and reflective. Leaders ask questions and seek answers. Leaders in education are familiar with current research and best practice, not only in education but also in other related fields. They maintain a personal plan for self-improvement and continuous learning and balance their professional and personal lives, making time for other interests.

9. Leaders have the courage to take informed risks.

Leaders embrace informed, planned change and recognize that everyone may not support change. Leaders work to win support and are willing to take action in support of their vision, even in the face of opposition.

About the Authors

Robert Ricken, EdD, served as principal and superintendent in the Mineola School District for twenty-two years and was interim superintendent in the following districts: Half Hollow Hills Central High School District, North Bellmore, Elmont, Bellmore, Smithtown Central School District, and the Bellmore-Merrick Central High School District. Presently, he teaches educational administration at Long Island University, C. W. Post.

Dr. Ricken has served as the Long Island coordinator for the Anti-Defamation League's A World of Difference Institute and conducted antibias workshops in more than one hundred school districts. In addition, he has been the chairman of the board of the Nassau Citizens Budget Committee, board officer of School Business Partnerships of Long Island, vice president of the Nassau County Superintendents Association, and president of Phi Delta Kappa, C. W. Post Chapter. Additionally, he served as an impartial hearing officer and a member of the American Arbitration Association. In this capacity, he has conducted 3020A, Section 75, and special education hearings.

Robert Ricken is the author of the following publications:

- *Love Me When I'm Most Unlovable*, National Association of Secondary School Principals, 1984
- *Book Two—The Kids' View*, National Association of Secondary School Principals, 1987
- *The RA Guide to Nassau County Schools*, Carlton Press, 1995
- *The Middle Level Calendar: A Handbook for Practitioners*, National Association of Secondary School Principals, 1996
- *The High School Principal's Calendar—A Month-by-Month Planner for the School Year*, Corwin Press, 2000
- *The Elementary School Principal's Calendar—A Month-by-Month Planner for the School Year*, Corwin Press, 2001

Dr. Ricken's other articles have been published in the *New York Times, Newsday, Sports Illustrated, The Harvard Review, Harper's Weekly,* and *Single Parent Magazine.* He is a frequent contributor to many educational journals and has written a column on education for a local newspaper, *Economic Times* of Long Island.

Dr. Ricken has presented many workshops and was recently the keynote speaker for the National Association of Secondary School Principals in New Orleans, the National Association of Middle Schools in West Virginia, Baltimore, Denver, Washington D.C., and Atlanta. He also has spoken at the National School Boards Association in San Francisco and Rochester, as well as for Phi Delta Kappa at Hofstra, C. W. Post, and Molloy College.

Awards include the Administrator of the Year by Phi Delta Kappa of Hofstra University, Administrator of the Year by Nassau-Suffolk Educator's Association, and recognition for his work in labor relations by the New York Council of Administrators and Supervisors. The National Public Relations Association honored him for his exemplary public relations practices. In 1992, he received the Outstanding Service Support Award from the Girl Scouts of Nassau County. In 1994, he was the recipient of the Dr. Martin Luther King, Jr. Recognition Award by Nassau County. In 2000, the New York State Middle School Association awarded him the Ross M. Burkhardt Award for his outstanding contribution to middle-level education.

Michael Terc, MA, PD, served as an administrator in the Mineola Public School District. For sixteen years, he served as assistant principal at Mineola High School in New York. Before that, he taught mathematics at Mineola Middle School for sixteen years. He also served as principal of the Mineola Summer School Program for two years. During his career, he coached many sports teams and was involved in a host of student activities. He served as president of the Nassau County Baseball Coaches Association and in 1976 was selected as the *Daily News'* High School Baseball Coach of the Year. In 1982, he authored "Coordinate Geometry and Art: A Match," published in *National Council of Mathematics Teachers Journal.* In 1994, he received the Jenkins Service Award, the highest service award given by the Mineola School District's PTA Association. He received his MA in mathematics from Hofstra University and was awarded a Professional Diploma in educational administration from Long Island University, C. W. Post campus. He recently was selected by the School Administrators Association of New York State to receive its 1999–2000 New York State Distinguished Assistant Principal of the Year Award. His most recent publication was *The Elementary School Principal's Calendar: A Month-by-Month Planner for the School Year.*

Chapter One

If it is to be, it is up to me.

—Unknown

When we speak about middle school administration, we rarely talk in the first person. The quote this month is an occasional necessity, even though we value a collaborative leadership style. The planning a principal does in the summer can be a lonely, but necessary, undertaking. Once completed, a feeling of self-satisfaction is legitimate, especially when our attention to every detail sets a positive tone for the forthcoming academic year.

A principal experiences a wide range of emotions after the school year ends. The satisfaction and exhilaration of the culminating activities are suddenly replaced by the loneliness of an empty building. As staff members rush off to their well-deserved vacations, the principal is left to close the books on the past semester and regenerate enthusiasm for the upcoming year. The authors liken the experience in July to a New Year's celebration. We look back on the previous twelve months and develop our resolutions for the coming year. We must radically switch gears to assure that all is ready for September. It is often an enormous, unilateral undertaking as indicated by our key tasks format.

To prevent personal burnout, the principal should take a vacation from mid-July to mid-August. We've discovered that vacationing at the end of August is counterproductive. Principals may be away from the job toward the end of August, but their minds will invariably revert to their unfinished school checklist. We cannot vacation when we are mentally back at our desks. Will we have time to complete everything before the first day of school? Almost instinctively our mind returns to an operational mode.

Perhaps it's too simplistic to describe July as an ending and August as a beginning since we must acknowledge the many important decisions that we made during the previous year's budgetary process: We have already planned for maintenance, textbooks, and educational priorities for the coming year; we probably have completed the master schedule, set up our teacher teams, and, hopefully, hired most of the new teachers and staff; and prior to going on vacation, we have closed the books on the past and have begun to concentrate on our new challenges.

We are compelled to mention summer school, which usually functions with a different principal. The recent trend toward standards-based education and concepts, such as No Child Left Behind, has created a proliferation of summer programs. We have observed that many school principals often abdicate their leadership and authority to an outside principal who manages summer school. An astute principal should make some demands on the summer school leadership team. Summer school principals must respect your facility, help educate your remedial students, and run a disciplinary tight ship. Remember, it's still your building and your children.

The nuts and bolts we describe in each monthly chapter are our professional responsibilities. We must set a positive tone so that our staff can become the driving force in implementing our educational plans. Ultimately, a framework for success is created. There is no substitute for a smooth opening to the school year. Staff members will become motivated when our organizational skills demonstrate that caring is an action word.

July Key Tasks

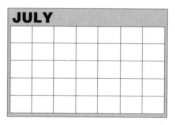

* *Monitor Summer School*

We advise principals to monitor the summer school operating in their building. Assist the summer school administrator by reviewing your disciplinary procedures so that your students do not sense a lowering of standards during summer school.

Make sure that final summer school grades are reported promptly, so your guidance staff can make the appropriate changes in student schedules. Monitor students' academic progress, especially the progress of those who were receiving special services during the regular school term. This is a two-way responsibility. Full-time staff members should describe services needed, and summer school teachers should provide instruction that meets individual students' needs.

Personal Commentary/Notes: _____

_____

Review Curriculum-Writing Projects ✳

Forward-thinking districts fund summer writing projects to update the curriculum. In a best-case scenario, the principal and his or her staff were involved in the development of improvement areas, and the principal invited qualified teachers to perform the tasks. This is not merely a means to offer staff members extra pay but an opportunity to effect positive changes into the curriculum. Your most knowledgeable and creative teachers should be encouraged to perform this vital function.

The principal should make sure that the finished product reaches the building staff at the start of school. Too often, projects developed over the summer are not duplicated in a timely fashion and are not made available until several months after their development. This is one time when compulsive leadership is encouraged.

Personal Commentary/Notes: _____

_____

Review Teacher Evaluations ✳

In an ideal situation, the principal will have written and delivered by the end of the school year each staff member's evaluation as well as set up their future goals. Knowing the hectic pace of June and the pressure of closing activities, the summer should be used to review each teacher's evaluation. Believe it or not, we have found that it's easier for principals to determine objectives for new and weaker staff members than for those receiving superior evaluations. We are competent when it comes to remediation, but often we don't know how to raise the bar for our finest professionals. Here are some ideas for the experts on your teaching staff:

1. Teach model lessons for new teachers

2. Serve on specific committees to make use of members' expertise

3. Become a mentor for a colleague

4. Undertake a curriculum revision project

5. Assist you during their building assignment, either with discipline or other administrative duties

For best results, invite certain staff members in during the summer to perform the evaluations in a calm environment. This makes the conference very meaningful, giving a pat on the back to the excellent teacher or providing a crucial meeting with a staff member whose job is in jeopardy.

Personal Commentary/Notes: _____

_____

* Meet With Custodial Staff

Arrange a meeting to include your head custodian and the supervisor of the district's buildings and grounds. Since both you and the supervisor will be evaluating the head custodian, the meeting should clearly set both leaders' expectations for summer work. A brief meeting with the district supervisor should precede the session, so you both have the same focus.

Every year, students and staff should return to a clean building and beautifully waxed floors. This should be a minimal expectation. A good custodial staff should also be able to paint hallways and several classrooms. They should be able to complete several minor construction projects, such as building bookcases, hanging wall maps, and refinishing furniture. The head custodian should provide a weekly progress report to both administrators. The principal should be notified immediately if any of the anticipated projects cannot be completed on time. The head custodian should exit the conference with the feeling that the entire staff is counting on his or her skills.

Personal Commentary/Notes: _____

_____

* Review and Revise Student Handbook

With computers, the process of revising the student handbook is more manageable. Most administrators maintain files on almost everything they do during the year. An assistant principal in a New York school district informed us that during the school year, she drops little notes into a file titled "Student Handbook Possible Changes," noting revisions or ideas for the upcoming year. In July, she reviews each new idea with the principal and reproduces a revised handbook.

In one year, she included a wording change in the school's mission statement; a board policy statement about the disciplinary code; an updated list of clubs, advisors, and new staff members; as well as new requirements for honor society induction. (See Resource 1: Student Handbook Topics.)

Personal Commentary/Notes: _____

_____

Update Teacher Manual *

As part of our orientation with new teachers, the last meeting evaluates the teacher manual. This helps to gauge the effectiveness of our work and update the information contained in the manual.

We also take a few minutes at a faculty meeting to get suggestions from experienced staff members. The faculty is told in advance to bring their manuals and any suggestions they may have to improve the product. This is usually a very fruitful meeting, and it demonstrates that we value teachers' input. (See Resource 2: Teacher Manual Topics.)

Personal Commentary/Notes: _____

_____

Review School Board's Policy Manual *

We recommend reviewing the manual with other principals or central office administrators. It's even more effective if the school board's attorney can be present. The goal is to find and review new items that affect employees. For example, in several states during the past few years, laws have been passed regarding reporting of child abuse, changes in mandated graduation requirements, changes in special education mandates, fingerprinting of prospective employees, and new requirements for licensing teacher aides and paraprofessionals.

Personal Commentary/Notes: _____

_____

Develop a Mission Statement *

A formal, written mission statement should be in place before any school improvement efforts are undertaken. This helps avoid a haphazard approach to school improvement in which numerous, sometimes conflicting efforts occur simultaneously. Ambiguous goals too often drain staff of their energy and motivation and yield no positive outcomes. Set a focus and stay the course. (See Resource 3: How to Build a Mission Statement for School Improvement.)

Personal Commentary/Notes: _____

_____

Review and Revise Administrative Responsibilities *

Depending on your staff, the reexamination of supervisory responsibilities is a critical component to your organization's success. We must look at things for the first time again. Recently, a principal in North Carolina mentioned to us that she hired a new assistant principal who had extraordinary skills in mathematics and computers. Although she had supervised the mathematics and computer areas in prior years, she reorganized the administrative responsibilities so that the new administrator could supervise those departments.

If you have chairpersons, coordinators, or team leaders, responsibilities should be clearly articulated and understood by all. Make certain that these school leaders have the legal right to supervise their colleagues. Usually, members of the teacher unit or a recognized union have a major loyalty conflict if they have to participate in the firing of a staff member. Consult official job descriptions to discover the rights and responsibilities of your fellow supervisors.

Personal Commentary/Notes: _____

_____

* Attend Monthly Board of Education Meetings

Middle schools often do not get equal time at board of education meetings. Parents of elementary children are usually very involved and often articulate their concerns. The high school has a status of its own since everyone is interested in high school students' activities and postgraduation placements. We feel it's incumbent on middle school principals to let the board and the community know about middle school activities. At the same time, we should educate the community about the goals of middle-level education.

Take every opportunity to share news about the staff, the children, and the school's activities. If possible, have a PTA member make a brief report at every board meeting. This is a critical segment of your public relations program and one that is often neglected.

Personal Commentary/Notes: _____

_____

* Analyze Trends in Disciplinary Referrals

Now is the time to review the number and types of disciplinary referrals that were received during the past school year. The number written by each teacher provides information that allows the principal to assist struggling teachers and provides a form of documentation for those who are not improving. Sending a teacher who needs additional strategies to a conference on discipline makes a great deal of sense.

Analyzing where infractions take place provides information for the staff, who can then review certain procedures. If the cafeteria is the place where infractions are most frequent, then perhaps staff members need more support in this area. We've found that assigning an administrator to monitor dismissal and arrival into the cafeteria dramatically reduces disciplinary referrals.

If one team of teachers is issuing most of the referrals, the principal should determine if the problems are attributable to a particular group of difficult children or if the team needs to be reconstituted the following year with the addition of a staff member who excels in student control. We say more about the constitution of teams later.

Personal Commentary/Notes: _____

_____

Examine School Statistics ✳

Too often principals wait for someone in the central office to apprise them of their students' results on standardized tests. We recommend the opposite. Principals should not only review all test data, but they also should both inform the superintendent of the test scores and provide a plan to improve any score that falls below the norm. This makes the central office staff confident about the principal's ability to plan remediation and demonstrates that the principal is on top of every situation.

Obviously, each team and each department must be involved in the evaluation of their own test results and should also participate in the development of the remediation plan. Remember, as principal, you want your staff members to have ownership of their plans.

Personal Commentary/Notes: _____

_____

Assess Each Department's Status ✳

Sometimes the team structure of middle schools overshadows the importance of the school's academic departments. Recent attacks on middle schools center around the belief that academics are de-emphasized and are deemed secondary to interdisciplinary, student-centered activities. Both aspects should be given credence and support. Poor academic results undermine everything else we're trying to do for children.

Regular meetings should be held with subject area supervisors throughout the year, but the July meeting is an essential element of planning and evaluation for the future. With academic results in hand, the principal and subject area leader should do the following:

1. Discuss the strengths and weaknesses of the department.

2. Review plans for remediation, if necessary.

3. Ensure that textbooks are current and will be available on the first day of the school year.

4. Review the curriculum and decide who will monitor the curriculum-writing project that might be undertaken during the summer. Remember, the goal is to have the revised curriculum ready and duplicated for the opening of school.

5. Evaluate each teacher and review each teacher's goals for the upcoming year. Some teachers may function better in the high school, and this, too, can be discussed.

Personal Commentary/Notes: _____

_____

* Review Team Assignments

Teams should be balanced, with staff members possessing teaching and nonteaching skills. Effective roles, such as being a cooperative team player, a disciplinarian, an organizational expert, or a subject specialist, are needed on each team. Sometime we have to dissolve an excellent team because we need a specific teacher's strength on a weaker team. On a rare occasion, we may have a particularly difficult group of children who need a team of teachers who are superior disciplinarians. We may decide to sacrifice some creativity to ensure an ordered academic environment for these young people. Setting up teams is truly a skill. Balance and purpose must be considered, and often decisions are based on the expertise or weakness of your staff.

We believe teams are the heart of the middle school. They provide a family structure and ensure that each child is well-known by several classroom teachers. Team planning periods allow staff members to create positive interdepartmental projects and also enable conferences about individual children to take place on a daily basis. Middle schools should be able to guarantee that no child will be neglected. Any student who is functioning poorly or who displays a radical change in behavior should be an immediate candidate for a case conference. Parents may be contacted to make certain there has not been a problem at home, or parents' help can be enlisted to provide support for plans that emerge from the meeting.

Personal Commentary/Notes: _____

_____

* Meet With Parents

These sessions should be both formal and informal. Regularly scheduled PTA meetings are a fixture of all schools. Unique to the middle-level principalship is the reaching out to the less-involved parents. Many economically deprived, single, and bilingual parents need special overtures. A principal in Rhode Island advertises in the local newspapers that he is available every summer morning to discuss personal problems. He asks parents to call in advance, if possible, to avoid meeting conflicts. He also lets people know he has Spanish and Portuguese interpreters available. Since some parents may not be able to stop in to see the principal in person, we suggest a letter be sent home regarding this matter. (See Resource 4: How Parents Can Help Their Children Succeed.)

A principal in Mineola, New York, asks parents of sixth graders, who are extremely nervous about entering the middle school, to have their children come into the building and work in the office during the summer. The secretary can schedule appropriate times if too many students are involved. The simple process of delivering mail and textbooks familiarizes them with the building and can go a long way toward reducing their anxieties.

Personal Commentary/Notes: _____

_____

Review District Calendar *

Although the principal has submitted the middle school input for inclusion in the district calendar, this is a good time to extract every date that is a priority for the building's staff. Double-check to see that the middle school received equal time on the calendar, which goes out to every resident of the district, and that all information is accurate.

On a more personal level, the middle school principal should review events such as art shows, concerts, and science fairs to be certain that they don't conflict with other activities. Field trips scheduled during examination times are a typical example of an inexcusable scheduling error.

Holiday activities and other annual events are easy to schedule, but, as you will see in this calendar, merely carrying forth the date can lead to terrible consequences. Recently, religious holidays for one minority group fell early in the year, and a major school activity had to be canceled due to a community furor. Lack of attention to detail often allows residents to feel we are not sensitive to their religious or ethnic community. If we fail to plan, we plan to fail.

Personal Commentary/Notes: _____

_____

Check Status of Purchase Orders *

Our goal is to have every item we ordered arrive prior to the start of school. Therefore, we send out our purchase orders prior to the budget vote. In this way, purchase orders can go out in January or February, marked for delivery on July 1. If the budget doesn't pass, we merely cancel the order. This is why our teachers always have their equipment and supplies before the start of the school year.

If purchase orders are not in the regular pipeline, we call vendors and make demands for action. Don't leave it to a clerk in the business office, since they are concerned about the entire district. Put your secretary or assistant principal on the alert to follow up on all purchase orders. If not, do it yourself.

Personal Commentary/Notes: _____

_____

* *Contact Local Police and Fire Officials*

Every school should have current disaster plans in the event of an emergency. Unfortunately, in contemporary America, violence, bomb threats, fire, and civil disturbances should be anticipated. In consultation with local law enforcement officers and school attorneys, the principals should learn their rights and responsibilities on a yearly basis since school law and local statutes change frequently. For example, in New York State, the principal may resume classes after searching a building during a bomb scare. However, once the building is emptied and police are called in, the students may not reenter without police (not the school principal's) approval. Good relations are helpful during these troubled and uncertain emergency situations. In this environment, caution is the watchword. Police professionalism should be respected, but the in loco parentis role of the principal is paramount. The students are, in the final analysis, our children.

Fire officials should be given equal time. State education departments require a specific number of fire drills each year. Most insist on a dozen, with approximately eight performed prior to December 31. Try to conduct practice fire drills during different periods, so students and staff learn the proper escape routes from different locations in the building. Fire officials should check alarm boxes and discuss response time in emergency situations. Principals should be aware that in a fire, casualties are dramatically increased if students take longer than two minutes to exit a building.

Such meetings foster good relations with two of the community's most important service organizations. In most rural and suburban districts, fire personnel are usually volunteers and often involve your students' older siblings and parents.

Personal Commentary/Notes: _____

_____

* *Review Report Cards and Grades*

Review the final report cards for accuracy and grading trends. Review individual teachers' class grades. Are they extreme, or do they reflect major unexplained changes in pattern or passing and failing statistics? This process might signal problems with individual staff members, departments, or the entire grading process.

Personal Commentary/Notes: _____

_____

July Communications

Write Letter to Staff *

This is an opportunity to show appreciation for the enormous effort your staff members put forth during the recently completed school year. Since you've already held individual evaluation sessions with each teacher, this communication is used to emphasize the staff members' cooperative efforts. This correspondence should bring a sense of pride to your teachers and serve as an additional warm send-off for their vacation period.

Most principals mention many of their schools' successes and highlight the accomplishments that were due to the dedication of the entire staff. We also think that an update of curriculum-writing projects should be included. This item has even greater significance if the design for the projects came from the expressed needs of the faculty.

Make teachers aware of building improvements and painting of classrooms or hallways. They appreciate hearing about new equipment, especially classroom teaching aids. It's a source of comfort for them to know that the physical plant is being improved while they're away.

In August, you'll write your welcome-back letter. For now, staff members deserve accolades for their past performance.

Personal Commentary/Notes: _____

_____

Develop a Public Relations Program *

Every school should have a public relations (PR) program. We have a responsibility to continually make residents aware of the middle school philosophy. The school's PR program may borrow from the district's effort, but there are a host of activities that are uniquely our own. When we asked middle school principals to list some of the components of such a program, we were amazed at the quality of their input. The following suggestions are from members of the New York State Middle School Principals Association:

1. Form a group of key communicators, made up of important members of your community and the media. Be sure to include PTA representatives. These key communicators should receive all PR correspondence and announcements of middle school events.

2. For parents:
   - Distribute a weekly newsletter.
   - Create a yearly packet of materials and distribute it to your PTA.
   - Regularly schedule meetings and office "teas."

3. With staff:
   - Distribute a newsletter.
   - Conduct faculty meetings.
   - Promote a sunshine committee to celebrate events and respond to hardships.

4. With students:
   - Issue daily PA announcements.
   - Meet with the school's student council.
   - Develop a student handbook.
   - Attend student activities.
   - Start a lunch club and meet with students of the month.

5. Miscellaneous:
   - Purchase a camera and post pictures of students and special activities in the main lobby.
   - Send birthday and holiday cards to students and staff.
   - Develop a school Web page.
   - Invite real estate agents, grandparents, and senior citizens to visit your school.
   - Send get-well cards to students who become hospitalized.

Personal Commentary/Notes: _____

_____

* Write Letter to Incoming Class

Middle school principals must anticipate the feelings of the children in the lowest grade. These children are coming from an elementary school they attended for six years and have become quite comfortable with that environment. Now they spend the summer awaiting a new school and children from other elementary schools. They are usually nervous about having so many teachers and being able to find all of their classrooms. This letter of welcome conveys to both the children and their parents that your staff will be doing everything to make the transition as comfortable as possible.

Mention some of the things that are being done in anticipation of their arrival. Let them know about teams and guidance counselors. A word about your availability in the event of any concern should do much to comfort everyone back home.

By all means, note the orientation dates and the welcome-back activities. Remind them that another letter will be sent to them at the end of August to inform them about their homeroom, their bus schedule, and the arrival time on the first day of school. We always ask students and parents to call if they have any questions, although many colleagues feel this causes many petty contacts from nervous parents.

Personal Commentary/Notes: _____

Write Letter to New Faculty and Staff Members *

Without meaning to insult new teachers, many have similar anxieties to those of our incoming students. They are eager to get started, decorate their rooms, receive a copy of the teacher manual and student handbook, and meet their colleagues. Your letter should describe the entire orientation program after you welcome them to your school. We believe in dedicating our first faculty meeting to a review of many of the things we know they'll need to be successful.

A good orientation program should include all of the items previously discussed, and supportive sessions should be planned throughout the year. Mentor teachers should be involved to add their expertise to the orientation process.

We think it's a good idea for new teachers to meet with school business officials, so they can review their benefits, pay schedules, health insurance, and payroll deductions, which will be taken out for such things as social security, taxes, and annuities. Filling out a host of forms could easily be completed when all of the new teachers are together. This will also help the efficiency of the business office.

This first letter should extend a warm welcome to the middle school family. Include a letter from your faculty sunshine committee or a union building representative as a means of reaching out to the newcomers. Providing new teachers with a copy of their schedules, curriculum outlines, and textbooks that relate to their courses will go a long way toward reducing their anxieties.

Personal Commentary/Notes: _____

Establish Membership in Civic Associations *

Students and schools benefit greatly from the principal's membership in local service organizations. Contacting the Rotary, Kiwanis, and Lions Clubs and the local chamber of commerce should also be part of the principal's PR initiative.

Club members are people who live and often work in the community, and telling them your story improves the image of the middle school. These members are also adults who often volunteer their time and can be role models for children.

Since it is nearly impossible for the principal to join all of these organizations, we urge you to encourage your assistants and key faculty members to become active in one or more of these groups. This action will serve to give the middle school a knowledgeable school PR person at all community events.

Personal Commentary/Notes: _____

_____

* *Subscribe to Local Newspapers*

In some communities, the local editor or newspaper owner allows each school in the district to submit columns for publication. This is a vital means of communicating with the entire population of your community, even those who do not have a child in your school. Getting someone to write the column is worth a building assignment if you are unable to do it yourself.

Subscribing to local papers is an excellent way to ensure that you will be informed about local civic activities and issues. Frequently, your school will be able to be part of a community celebration. A relationship with a local paper is a worthwhile partnership to foster.

Personal Commentary/Notes: _____

_____

* *Write Letter to Nonpublic Schools*

Each July, we write a note to every nonpublic school in our community to inform them about our school's yearly activities. We frequently invite them to come to our school to hear an outstanding speaker or perhaps watch a vendor present a demonstration of a new educational product. It is to our advantage if the private schools use the same textbooks and curriculum as our schools, since many students transfer into our public schools during the year.

Should a community disaster occur, we should have positive working relationships with all school leaders. Also, with new laws on sex offenders, we must inform each other and our residents when a released child predator moves into the neighborhood. We are all partners in our effort to protect children and keep our hometown safe.

Personal Commentary/Notes: _____

_____

Write Letter to Parents Suggesting ✱
Summer Activities for Students

Parents appreciate suggestions for summer activities. Include a note to parents with the final report card informing them of summer projects that will supplement learning activities throughout the school year. Keeping a summer diary, writing to pen pals, sketching while traveling, collecting items (rocks, shells, coins, stamps, etc.), and playing educational games are some examples of productive educational summer activities. A summer reading list prepared by the school media specialist and produced in conjunction with the local library provides another useful project.

Personal Commentary/Notes: _____

July Planning

Finalize New Student ✱
Orientation Program

We recommend bringing in the new sixth-grade class the week prior to the start of school. During a two-hour block of time, the students are given their homeroom assignments, so they know where to report the first day of school. They are also taught how to use a combination lock. Arrange to have current student leaders talk to them about the extracurricular activities they can join. Showing a video of the previous year's events can be quite motivational. Conduct a question-and-answer period with counselors and school administrators at the end of the orientation to address any lingering anxieties.

Follow the orientation with a barbecue, with staff and students intermingling in a picnic atmosphere. This is a special activity that can be cosponsored by the school's parent organization. It helps set the family tone that is encouraged throughout the year.

Personal Commentary/Notes: _____

Conduct Administrative Team Workshop ✱

Review all school rules as well as every aspect of the opening of school. We also discuss the staffing of each department and the makeup of every team. All administrative responsibilities are assigned at the meeting, and the supervision of new teachers is delegated.

This is a time when all concerns should be aired so that the future year will be addressed by a coordinated supervisory team. We often talk about teacher teams but neglect to mention that the school's administrators should function in the same manner.

Personal Commentary/Notes: _____

_____

* Finalize Calendar for Field Trips and Fundraising Activities

To avoid conflicts, field trips should not be scheduled when examinations are being given. We stop all field trips a month and a half before the end of school to avoid a conflict with teachers who are reviewing their year's work. We also want to encourage a serious end-of-year tone.

Organizations doing fundraising should not be in competition with each other. We require such activities to be planned and approved in advance, so we can put them on the school calendar.

Personal Commentary/Notes: _____

_____

July Personnel

* Review Staffing and Tenure Recommendations

The finalization of all faculty positions should be closely monitored. Any opening should be posted and advertised, and arrangements should be made for summer interviews. This process should be followed for all support staff as well.

We believe that all cocurricular positions should also be filled as early as possible. This contributes to a smooth opening for these activities in September. It also enables faculty advisors to plan over the summer.

A final check should also be made of contractual obligations. Timelines should be followed for staff members who are scheduled for appointment to tenure. A similar review should be made for the nonteaching staff (secretaries, clerks, aides, monitors, etc.), particularly in states where they are governed by civil service law. Some states have a form of tenure after a brief probationary period.

Personal Commentary/Notes: _____

_____

July Checklists

July Key Tasks

Major Assignments	Date Started	Date Completed	Days on Task
Monitor summer school			
Review curriculum-writing projects			
Review teacher evaluations			
Meet with custodial staff			
Review and revise student handbook			
Update teacher manual			
Review school board's policy manual			
Develop a mission statement			
Review and revise administrative responsibilities			
Attend monthly board of education meetings			
Analyze trends in disciplinary referrals			
Examine school statistics			
Assess each department's status			
Review team assignments			
Meet with parents			
Review district calendar			
Check status of purchase orders			
Contact local police and fire officials			
Review report cards and grades			

July Communications

✓	Assignment
	Write letter to staff
	Develop a public relations program
	Write letter to incoming class
	Write letter to new faculty and staff members
	Establish membership in civic associations
	Subscribe to local newspapers
	Write letter to nonpublic schools
	Write letter to parents suggesting summer activities for students

July Planning

✓	Assignment
	Finalize new student orientation program
	Conduct administrative team workshop
	Finalize calendar for field trips and fundraising activities

July Personnel

✓	Assignment
	Review staffing and tenure recommendations
	Finalize faculty positions and teaching schedules
	Finalize rosters for all other staff positions
	Appoint extracurricular advisorships
	Finalize coaching assignments

July Calendar

MONTH: JULY

YEAR: ____

MONDAY	TUESDAY	WEDNESDAY	THURSDAY	FRIDAY	SATURDAY
					SUNDAY
MONDAY	TUESDAY	WEDNESDAY	THURSDAY	FRIDAY	SATURDAY
					SUNDAY
MONDAY	TUESDAY	WEDNESDAY	THURSDAY	FRIDAY	SATURDAY
					SUNDAY
MONDAY	TUESDAY	WEDNESDAY	THURSDAY	FRIDAY	SATURDAY
					SUNDAY
MONDAY	TUESDAY	WEDNESDAY	THURSDAY	FRIDAY	SATURDAY
					SUNDAY

NOTES

20

Chapter Two

No school will ever become a model of excellence with the bland leading the bland.

—Robert Ricken

Our key tasks are now designed for time-sensitive action. Each item on our to-do list will help get the school year started in an efficient manner. Although the opening of school varies by state, the ideas and strategies are transferable to relevant dates in each school system.

The middle school principal now has to process the information he or she has received from the site-based teams and from the school improvement committee. Many members of these groups might be available for consultation in the days prior to the opening of school. We encourage these contacts, which foster ownership and mobilize staff members to assist in achieving the goals for the start of school. The middle school is a "we-our-ours-us" institution, which rejects the "I-my-mine-me" mentality.

We polled dozens of principals throughout the country and asked them to share with us some of the unique activities they perform during the weeks prior to the opening of school. Here are some of their ideas:

1. A principal from Utah invites some overly frightened sixth graders to come to the office to assist him and the secretarial staff. They deliver mail and texts to teacher classrooms, but more important, they become familiar with the facility, which helps lessen their anxieties.

2. We learned that a Texas principal invites new teachers in for a coffee hour, during which he shows them their rooms, distributes the teacher manual,

answers their questions, and tells them to expect a call from one of their experienced team members. Obviously, he has requested the cooperation of his senior staff members in advance.

3. A California principal invites her cafeteria aides in before the start of school so that they are prepared for all of the routines she wants implemented from Day 1.

4. Several principals we talked to meet with team leaders to discuss school activities, including interdepartmental projects, field trips, and ways to assist each other with discipline and creative scheduling.

5. Several principals discussed their strategy of inviting PTA members in to plan the entire year's schedule of meetings, so they can add them to the teacher, student, and parent handbooks.

One of our requests is that all bus drivers perform a dry run of their route. The bus drivers also receive discipline cards to turn in daily, so any misbehavior on a bus can be handled immediately by our staff. This helps the drivers know we are concerned about safety and are supporting them.

In the middle of the month, the principal or his or her staff should check the public address system, fire extinguishers, and fire drill signs and conduct a final tour of the entire building with the head custodian. The latter is most important, since summer school programs detract from the time custodians have to paint, polish, and do basic maintenance. Resource 5 includes items our custodians should be responsible for completing. (See Resource 5: Building Inspection Checklist.)

If you've had a productive summer, the school opening will bring pride to the entire staff. A famous Chinese philosopher, Lao Tsu, said:

The wicked leader is he who the people despise.

The good leader is he who the people revere.

The great leader is he whose people say, . . . We did it ourselves.

The truth is, if the staff members were involved in the decision-making process and are truly part of the team, they deserve much of the credit. In their eyes, you are their leader, not their boss.

The following poem expresses our sentiments on this subject.

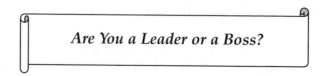

Are You a Leader or a Boss?

The Boss drives the staff: The Leader coaches them.

The Boss depends upon authority: The Leader on good will.

The Boss inspires fear: The Leader inspires enthusiasm.

The Boss says, "I": The Leader says, "We."

The Boss assigns tasks: The Leader sets the pace.

The Boss says, "Get here on time": The Leader gets there ahead of time.

The Boss fixes the blame for the breakdown: The Leader fixes the breakdown.

The Boss knows how it is done: The Leader shows how it is done.

The Boss makes work a drudgery: The Leader makes it a game.

The Boss says, "Go": The Leader says, "Let's go."

The world needs Leaders—nobody needs a Boss.

AUGUST

August Key Tasks

*Prepare School Opening ∗
Remarks for Staff*

Just as we expect teachers to make an excellent first impression with their classes, we view the principal's opening remarks as an opportunity to inspire. This speech should be carefully written and not informal. The presentation should include many subtopics of major themes, such as expression of appreciation for past efforts, a welcome to new staff members, a review of the disciplinary process, a review of the first day's expectations for each teacher, a review of legal mandates, a presentation of summer curriculum projects, an overview of the faculty handbook, and a description of numerous teacher responsibilities. If these items are not covered in the principal's remarks, they must be handled at department or team meetings later in the day.

As you can readily note, the scope of this presentation is limitless. Here are the details of each of the topics that should be discussed. As with everything else in this calendar, we expect you to add items required for your particular situation and delete those that can be addressed at a later time.

1. Express your appreciation for the faculty's past efforts and list some major accomplishments made during the past year.

2. Assert your hope that their well-deserved rest served as a time of energy renewal.

3. Allow mentors or chairpersons to introduce new staff members and tell a little about their personal lives or experiences.

4. Review summer projects and distribute copies of new curriculum additions.

5. Review legal matters, such as child abuse responses; fire drill procedures; emergency security measures since September 11, 2001; locker search regulations; smoking prohibitions; and laws against corporal punishment.

6. Read the school's mission statement and mention that the entire faculty was involved in its development.

7. Review minimum requirements for getting the year started:
   - Review disciplinary code and procedures.
   - Highlight critical sections of the teacher manual and the student handbook.
   - Discuss classroom expectations for the first day of school.

8. Provide reminders for first homeroom:
   - Distribute student schedules.
   - Distribute locker assignments. Make sure new students are shown their lockers and are taught how to open a combination lock at some point before the first day of classes.
   - Take attendance and fill out emergency home contact cards.
   - Distribute an Internet usage agreement for student and parent signature.
   - Discuss absence notes and lateness procedures.

9. Review teacher responsibilities:
   - Define legal requirements of attendance procedures.
   - Discuss lesson plan expectations.
   - Define grading procedures.
   - Explain signing-in and signing-out procedures.
   - Discuss building assignments and duty periods.
   - Relate call-in procedure in the event of teacher absence.

Personal Commentary/Notes: _____

_____

* Meet With All Supervisors

This meeting enables the principal to both give and receive direction. Obviously, we wish to receive the supervisors' input for our opening remarks to the faculty. At the same time, we review their agenda items for their own meetings. We can use a checklist as mentioned previously to share responsibility for certain items and be certain that we are not duplicating our efforts. If we expect the staff members to coordinate their efforts, our opening meetings should be models for them to emulate.

In this meeting, the principal has an opportunity to learn if there are any problems or urgent needs noted by the department heads, team leaders, or assistant principals. Each supervisor should make a full report on the readiness of his or her department. We have always verbalized our expectation that each supervisor visits every classroom used by his or her staff. Books should be awaiting the children and distributed on the first day of school. We are also firm about giving some homework the first day of classes. In addition, we expect that all texts will be brought in with book covers by the second day of classes. We make no apology for these strict procedures and details.

The goals for each department head were probably determined during their previous year's evaluation. They should be reaffirmed at this time. If there is a new supervisor, time must be allocated during the summer to meet, to review staff members, and to set goals. Remember, supervisors also need an inspirational comment or two. We want them to start the year with specific objectives and renewed passion and energy.

Personal Commentary/Notes: _____

_____

Complete Master Schedule *

This is a time to do a check of every teacher's schedule, classroom assignments, and homeroom staffing. Where teachers have to share rooms, the principal should minimize the distance between classrooms. Wherever possible, give your new staff members a schedule that will enhance their chances to succeed. Often, new staff members are given too much work to prepare and a difficult building assignment, which can be counterproductive.

Personal Commentary/Notes: _____

_____

Review the School's Mission Statement *

This is a good time to review, affirm, or revise the mission statement. This practice will help parents, staff, and students focus their energies and efforts for the coming year. Included in the resource section (Resource 3) is an excellent article on how to develop a mission statement, if your school hasn't accomplished this task.

Personal Commentary/Notes: _____

_____

* Register New Students

Many states are quite strict with residency requirements for local school attendance. The secretary or registrar should receive the inservice training necessary to perform this task. Someone, preferably a counselor or administrator, must monitor classroom counts as each new student is registered. Doing this eliminates the balancing of classes after the start of the school year.

Personal Commentary/Notes: _____

_____

* Conduct Final Walk-Through With Head Custodian

The principal provides an extra set of eyes for assessing the work of the custodial staff. The building may be clean, but the principal's expertise is necessary to discover items that may affect the smooth opening of school. Special consideration is given to potential safety hazards. After we discussed final walk-throughs at a middle school conference, a principal from Florida who attended the conference mailed to us the following oversights she discovered in her August final check:

1. Fire exits were not all posted.
2. There were no garbage cans in the cafeteria.
3. Stairwell lights were not operating on one side of the building.
4. Three classrooms were missing desks.
5. The intercom system was not operating in the auditorium and cafeteria.
6. Three classroom teachers were missing classroom keys.
7. American flags were needed in several rooms.
8. Wastepaper baskets were missing on one entire floor.

These items may appear to be petty, but if thoroughness is our objective, we must do our part to avoid unnecessary distractions. Administrators are responsible for minimizing factors that adversely affect the smooth opening of school.

Personal Commentary/Notes: _____

_____

* Complete Last-Minute Double Checks

Following the walk-through with the custodian, the principal should develop his or her own list of items that could cause problems during the first day of classes. A final check of the following items is a part of the principal's Day 1 lesson plan:

1. Are the intercom system and bell system ready?

2. Are all fire extinguishers inspected and operable?

3. Are all emergency systems in order (e.g., first-aid kits replenished, exit lights operational, fire drill routes posted, and teacher keys in place)?

4. Are all lockers cleaned and repaired, and have replacement locks arrived for sale to students?

5. Does each classroom have supplies, texts, chalk, and erasers?

6. Are computers and audiovisual material operational?

Personal Commentary/Notes: _____

_____

August Communications

*Prepare Board of ***
Education Presentation

If given the opportunity to address the board of education, the middle school principal has an excellent public relations (PR) opportunity. At the very least, principals can praise students and staff.

Bringing in examples of excellent student work and unique faculty contributions secures support from the leaders of the district. Don't miss the chance to help the board and residents better understand the middle school experience.

Distribute the student handbook or a copy of the PTA meeting schedule, so board members and residents have something to take home after the meeting. This can serve to improve the image of your school.

Personal Commentary/Notes: _____

_____

*Meet With Parent-Teacher Association Leaders ***

At this meeting, the principal creates a cordial working relationship with parent leaders. The meeting provides a good opportunity to review the mission statement and remind everyone about the goals of middle-level education. This is the time to reserve the dates for all PTA meetings. Further discussion might even develop the tentative topics for each meeting. Input by the general membership should also be considered to set up meaningful programs. Membership drives should be finalized with a goal of reaching as many parents as possible. Be sure to inform school leaders about the first Open School Night, so they can share in the advertisement for the event.

Personal Commentary/Notes: _____

_____

✳ *Complete School Opening Memo for Staff*

Hold a meeting with your key supervisors and secretary to review old files and get input for additional items. This meeting is the first step in creating a school opening memo. Many of the staff responsibilities appear in the teachers' manual, but organizing them in this opening memo helps get everyone on the same page. In this memo, we stress activities that should occur during the first day's homeroom and subject periods:

1. Remind everyone about the day's bell schedule since the first day requires a prolonged homeroom to accomplish tasks listed under Item 2.

2. First homeroom information:
   • Distribute student schedules. Explain room locations to sixth graders.
   • Have students fill out emergency home contact cards.
   • Take attendance.
   • Discuss the requirement of notes for absences.
   • Distribute locker assignments and help sixth graders locate lockers.
   • Review routines, such as taking homeroom attendance, reciting the Pledge, and remaining quiet during announcements.

3. First class session reminders:
   • Discuss curriculum sequence.
   • Review disciplinary procedures.
   • Outline homework requirements.
   • Distribute books and require a protective cover.
   • Teach a mini-lesson.
   • Discuss class regulations.
   • Discuss grading and examination requirements.

4. Make certain you know your duty assignment and report promptly.

5. Know the date of the first preannounced fire drill and review with all classes the procedures to be followed.

Personal Commentary/Notes: _____

_____

Review Interim Reports *

Informing parents about their child's progress five weeks after the beginning of each quarter is a vital part of the school's communication program. Principals should hold sessions during the school year to review the printed formats and make revisions, so they are more meaningful for parents. We recommend that these interim reports be translated into foreign languages if your school has a non-English-speaking community.

Included in the resource section is a copy of an excellent interim report. Feel free to share this with your faculty and add or delete items as needed. Remember, different subjects have different needs, so faculty input is essential. (See Resource 6: Sample Interim Progress Report.)

The fourth interim report must be sent after the fourth week of the quarter, since it warns parents that their child may fail a course. When in doubt, teachers are asked to send this notification; doing so avoids a confrontation with outraged parents who feel they were never informed about this possibility. It is probably the most crucial communication between parent and school. Discuss interim reports at your April and June faculty meetings, and make them an item in the new teacher orientation program.

Personal Commentary/Notes: _____

_____

Send Letters to Students With Schedules for Opening Day *

It makes sense to send these letters out a week or two before the start of school to avoid numerous phone calls requesting the same information. Some of our colleagues simply include the homeroom assignments because they don't want to be deluged by requests for teacher changes. This is another opportunity to welcome students and enhance your PR program by adding a few positive items about the school's accomplishments.

Some principals we talked to at a recent middle school conference say they include the following information:

1. Bus schedules

2. Names of counselors

3. A list of extracurricular activities

4. The first student council event

5. A form to join the PTA

Personal Commentary/Notes: _____

_____

* Send Opening-of-School Letter to Faculty and Staff

This is another opportunity to extend both a welcome to staff and thanks for their efforts during the previous year. We hope they had a well-deserved rest and are enthusiastic about the coming semester. Many principals list the previous year's accomplishments and mention some summer highlights, such as curriculum enhancements and building renovations. It's helpful for the staff to receive the schedule for the first day.

Personal Commentary/Notes: _____

_____

* Send Letter to Parents About Future PTA Meetings

The principal and the PTA president should draft a letter to parents including dates and times for all PTA meetings and a listing of the topics to be discussed. Sometimes meeting topics in the letter can be designated with TBA—to be announced—with the explanation that input from all parents is desired at the first meeting. Forms for joining the PTA should be included, along with information about where to bring the envelopes and membership fee. In many buildings, this collection is done by a parent sitting outside the main office, which minimizes teacher involvement during the busy school opening days.

Personal Commentary/Notes: _____

_____

* Write Article for Student Newspaper

The first issue of the school newspaper should include pictures and brief biographies of new staff members. The principal has an added PR opportunity with this article because the paper also goes to students' homes. The article allows the school leader to publicize student and faculty achievements as well as forthcoming events.

Personal Commentary/Notes: _____

_____

* Prepare First Weekly Memo to Staff

This regular correspondence serves to organize the entire faculty. If future events are added at the bottom of each memorandum, it informs everyone about field trips, testing days, assemblies, and holidays and helps avoid scheduling conflicts. Event notifications can be publicized a month in advance and be included in each of the following week's memoranda.

This first letter should include many items involved in the start of school. Some principals mentioned to us that they use the September memo to reinforce school disciplinary rules, safety procedures, and important topics for the first homeroom and the first academic class session. A listing is made of all items to be turned in to the office, such as first day's attendance, health records, emergency home contact cards, and locker assignments. The memo should be designed to meet the organizational needs of the principal and staff.

Personal Commentary/Notes: _____

_____

Send Letter to Police, *
Fire Officials, and Local Politicians

The first items the principal wants to share with police, fire officials, and local politicians are the starting date and time schedule for the new school year. Police often assign crossing guards to busy intersections to assist with students who walk to school. Fire departments are informed about the first two fire drills and often are invited to the middle school to observe and critique them. Many communities have volunteer fire departments that usually involve students' family members. Both the fire department and the police also put up safety signs throughout the community announcing the opening of school.

Personal Commentary/Notes: _____

_____

Submit Grade Examination and Analysis *

Reviewing data is an ongoing responsibility of the principal. Part of the staff's responsibility in the grading process is to perform a thorough review of grades. An analysis should be done by meeting individually with each department leader to discuss the results of final examinations, standardized tests, and state assessments. Testing has become more prevalent throughout the nation in this era of accountability. Reviewing the results of examinations affords us the opportunity to monitor the instructional program. Performing an item analysis might inform us of our effectiveness in teaching a particular topic, or whether we are teaching a topic that is not part of our curriculum. In contemporary American schools, testing and comparing results with other schools and districts is a reality principals must acknowledge. Furthermore, understanding testing and being able to articulate the results is an additional skill that must be developed by the principal.

Personal Commentary/Notes: _____

_____

August Planning

* Establish Field Trip Schedule

Out-of-school trips should support classroom instruction. They should not be vacation days, since the children are missing several other classes when they leave the building. At minimum, teachers should detail how the trip will impact their curriculum. Follow-up activities should also be presented with the field trip application.

Field trips should be planned to avoid conflicts with other teachers and departments. Weekly memos to staff should include a section of upcoming events. Field trips must be listed at least two weeks prior to the event so that conflicts can be minimized and adjustments made. Curtailing field trips six weeks before the end of the school year is helpful to maintain a businesslike tone until moving-up exercises are held.

Personal Commentary/Notes: _____

_____

* Establish Fire Drill Schedule

There should be a fire drill during the first few days of school. Announce the drill in advance and give strict expectations to the students over the public address system. Another drill should be held a few days later, without prior notice. Fire department officials note that if it takes more than two minutes to evacuate a building during a real fire, casualties can be expected. This procedure must be viewed as a major safety event. Many states mandate as many as twelve drills a year, eight of which must be held before the winter recess. With security a major concern throughout the country, drills of any kind should be viewed as an operational mandate.

Personal Commentary/Notes: _____

_____

* Establish Goals and Special Projects

These determinations should be the result of all your meetings with supervisors, teachers, parents, and students. Their implementation will demonstrate the collective vision of your school community.

Determining goals and projects also indicates that we believe in the improvement process and resist resting on past laurels. The same expectation that we have for every staff member should be one of our own priorities. These goals may be short-term goals or multiyear expectations. A good example of a short-term goal might be to measure the number of cuts or discipline cards from last year to the conclusion of the present year to determine if our disciplinary plan is paying dividends. Some of the principal's projects that follow incorporate short- and long-term goals.

Specifying projects and prioritizing them should provide attainable objectives that enhance your supervisory model, curriculum, or facility. A principal from Connecticut formulated the following projects recently and reported that each was completed in a single school year:

1. Revise the health curriculum and secure the approval of the superintendent and the board of education.

2. Rewrite the portion of the disciplinary code dealing with lateness to class to reduce the problems perceived by staff concerning this matter.

3. Institute a new site-based management team to address the community's request to revise our local graduation requirements.

4. Establish a student-faculty committee to ensure consistency in the selection of students for extracurricular activities and establish an equitable process for excluding them from participation.

5. Complete the following facility improvement endeavors:
   a. Construct bookshelves in all social studies classrooms.
   b. Construct bulletin boards for the physical education department.
   c. Add electrical outlets in rooms 212, 214, 305 and in all science labs.
   d. Construct a small basement area to house records of students who graduated prior to 1985.
   e. Construct shelves in the in-school suspension room and stock them with the required texts from each department.
   f. Remove graffiti and paint both portable classrooms and all outside storage sheds.
   g. Reline all parking spots and fill in all potholes prior to the spring recess.

Personal Commentary/Notes: _____

_____

August Personnel

Set Shared Decision-Making *
Committee Meeting Dates

Many states now require shared decision-making committees, which include teachers, parents, and students. Some decision-making committees are mandated by law, and others have been negotiated by teachers' unions. As middle school administrators, we endorse the concept of shared decision making. Texts on management, both in schools and in the private sector, extol the virtue of collective management. Setting these dates at the beginning of the year indicates its importance and helps staff and parents, who are involved in many other activities, reserve the time and dates in their personal calendars.

Personal Commentary/Notes: _____

_____

✽ *Revise Staff Directory*

Every staff member should have the names and addresses of colleagues who work in the same building. We include the secretaries, aides, security personnel, cafeteria workers, custodians, and faculty. This helps during emergencies and when sending hospitality messages.

Personal Commentary/Notes: _____

_____

✽ *Review Substitute Teacher Procedures*

When substitute teachers cannot control their classes, the building's disciplinary tone is seriously compromised. Administrators from the Mineola Middle School in New York State have shared with us some helpful procedures they have developed to assist substitute teachers with discipline and to evaluate their effectiveness with students. We have included an assignment sheet that helps the substitute to know the rules of the school, a report that is submitted by the substitute at the end of the day, and a report by the absent teacher for completion upon his or her return to school. (See Resource 7: Middle School Substitutes' Memorandum.)

Students are told that if their names are reported by a substitute teacher, they will face serious disciplinary consequences. Substitutes are thus empowered by the form they are required to submit to the principal at the end of the day. Students quickly learn that if their regular teacher is absent, they must still behave properly in class.

Another helpful requirement is that all teachers must submit two canned lessons at the beginning of the year. These are used when absent teachers have an emergency and cannot leave plans. These support systems for substitute teachers encourage substitutes to add their names to the school's substitute availability list.

Personal Commentary/Notes: _____

_____

Complete New Teacher Orientation Plans *

Although we met with new teachers in July and started our orientation, now is the time to plan bimonthly meetings, preferably for the first semester. Material such as the teacher manual, schedules, duty assignments, and student handbook should have been distributed when the teacher was hired or at the July orientation meeting. The following additional tasks should be considered:

- Meet with administrators about lesson plan requirements.
- Review disciplinary procedures and make suggestions about how to handle such problems as talking in class, not doing homework, and cutting class.
- Set up meetings with subject area supervisors to review curriculum, testing mandates, and grading procedures.
- Arrange meeting with business officials to review pay periods, payroll deductions, health insurance coverage, and salary for extracurricular activities supervision.
- Prepare new teachers for Open School Night.
- Provide orientation for interim reports, report cards, and homeroom attendance mandates.
- Meet with faculty mentors to discuss teaming process and potential help for new colleagues.
- Discuss supervision and classroom observations.

Personal Commentary/Notes: _____

_____

August Checklists

August Key Tasks

Major Assignments	Date Started	Date Completed	Days on Task
Prepare school opening remarks for staff			
Meet with all supervisors			
Complete master schedule			
Review the school's mission statement			
Register new students			
Conduct final walk-through with head custodian			
Complete last-minute double checks			

August Communications

✓	Assignment
	Prepare board of education presentation
	Meet with parent-teacher association leaders
	Complete school opening memo for staff
	Review interim reports
	Send letters to students with schedules for opening day
	Send opening-of-school letter to faculty and staff
	Send letter to parents about future PTA meetings
	Write article for student newspaper
	Prepare first weekly memo to staff
	Send letter to police, fire officials, and local politicians
	Submit grade examination and analysis

August Planning

✓	Assignment
	Establish field trip schedule
	Establish fire drill schedule
	Establish goals and special projects

August Personnel

✓	Finalize
	Set shared decision-making committee meeting dates
	Revise staff directory
	Review substitute teacher procedures
	Complete new teacher orientation plans
	Fill remaining faculty/staff positions
	Review and update substitute teacher list

August Calendar

MONTH: AUGUST

YEAR: _____

MONDAY	TUESDAY	WEDNESDAY	THURSDAY	FRIDAY	SATURDAY
					SATURDAY ____
					SUNDAY ____
					SATURDAY ____
					SUNDAY ____
					SATURDAY ____
					SUNDAY ____
					SATURDAY ____
					SUNDAY ____
					SATURDAY ____
					SUNDAY ____

NOTES

_____

Chapter Three

September

High achievement always takes place in the framework of high expectations.

—Jack Kinder

A calm and orderly opening of school is not accidental or a matter of good fortune. It represents the evidence of excellent planning based on past experience and the organizational expertise of a competent principal. After every school opening, the building administrator should have the entire staff evaluate all of the activities used to start the year. This serves to improve the process for the following year. The principal, who values the staff's input, should place all suggestions in a file titled "Opening Procedures" for future consideration. In this case, having two files—one for September and one for opening procedures—is very helpful.

The long list of September tasks can seem intimidating initially. The tasks are not only numerous but are also open-ended. Furthermore, each item often generates numerous subtopics. The sheer number of responsibilities can overwhelm a new principal. The seasoned administrator understands that certain jobs must be delegated, whereas others are planned cooperatively, and some require the principal's personal attention. For each item mentioned, the principal might want to consider who is best able to be primarily responsible for coordinating the activity.

Sometimes at the start of the school year, we recommend that the principal remind the staff about two often-overlooked issues. The first is the characteristics of middle school children, which should be part of the teacher manual. We want our faculty members to consider these traits when planning their lessons and activities. The second issue is the concerns parents have about their children who are entering the middle school. Their concerns, or desires, could serve as our expectations for our school and staff. (See Resource 8: Characteristics of the Middle School Child.)

A principal in Utah, John H. Childs, once said:

> I believe our schools ought to be . . .
>
> Like Harvard—with a strong academic curriculum,
>
> Like West Point—with excellent discipline,
>
> Like Disneyland—with organized, positive excitement for children.

Let's take a moment to examine our parents' desires, in their own words:

1. First, and most important, we want our children in a safe environment.

2. We want our children to be known by several members of the staff.

3. We expect the staff members to encourage children to have healthy relationships with their peers, and we expect the staff to eliminate scapegoating and bullying.

4. We want the staff to provide our children with wholesome experiences and activities.

5. We want the school to inculcate a love of learning.

6. We want to know that our children are being prepared for success in high school.

7. While our children are in school, we want teachers to inform us about their progress.

8. When we visit the school, we would like to feel welcomed by the staff.

9. As parents, we would like to be part of the school's decision-making process.

10. We want to be further educated about the philosophy of middle-level education.

As you've probably noted, the parents' desires are tantamount to many of our own goals. Sharing these with your faculty will serve as a review for why most of us teach in the middle school. One principal had her staff list how they would respond to each of the parents' items by giving specific examples from their everyday practice. Both the middle school student characteristics and the parents' desires provide an excellent learning experience for new teachers and a needed reminder for veteran staff members. Discussion of these concerns can provide an excellent inservice at the start of the school year.

You will find that several of your September key tasks were enumerated in August. As each task is successfully completed, your intensive planning efforts and the sleepless nights you experienced during the two weeks prior to the opening of school will be justified.

SEPTEMBER

September Key Tasks

Conduct First Faculty Meeting *

This meeting sets the tone for the school year. Combine the required opening-of-school information with a review of all procedures developed to ensure an excellent academic tone. The items discussed not only are essential for your new staff members but also serve as a necessary review for your veterans. In September, there are fifteen major key tasks to consider. Make sure to introduce new staff members, review state-mandated topics, highlight the teacher manual, and review safety procedures. The specific requirements of the first day of classes are a top priority. Again, thanking the staff for past efforts and sharing an inspirational story adds the human touch you want to accompany the strict intensity of the opening procedures.

Since this meeting is usually followed by department and team meetings, it is a challenge to accomplish all of the agenda items. It might be wise to have some of them covered by the department chairpersons or by memoranda. The experienced principal should also be aware that teachers want more than anything to get into their classrooms to complete their own preparations.

Personal Commentary/Notes: _____

_____

Review Opening Preparations *

Each principal should have a list of last-minute things to check. Some tasks can be done by an assistant principal, head custodian, or a member of the secretarial staff. Check the items under Last-Minute Double Checks in the August Key Tasks against your own items. Pay particular attention to the first day's agenda. For example, mentally walk through the day:

1. Do students know where their homerooms are?

2. Do homeroom teachers have a schedule for each child?

3. Have you reviewed the homeroom teachers' responsibilities?

4. Do classroom teachers have texts and class lists?

5. Are cafeteria workers prepared to establish routines for students?

6. Are cooks ready with a simple first-day menu?

7. Have bus drivers been properly oriented, and do they know their routes?

8. Do you have a list of items that homeroom and classroom teachers should turn in at the end of the day (e.g., health forms, emergency home contacts, problems with texts)?

Personal Commentary/Notes: _____

_____

* Meet With Staff to Discuss Security Plans

Since the September 11, 2001, terrorist attacks, security has become a priority for all public and private institutions. Many schools never had security guards and simply had staff members cover key areas with building assignments. Today, whether the district has authorized the employment of security personnel or not, the principal is responsible for developing a security plan.

The usual concerns, such as fire drills and securing the building from intruders, are now supplemented with policies to deal with chemical spills, bomb scares, false alarms, weapons, fireworks, child predators, and legal guardianship of students. The last issue has burgeoned along with the divorce rate and the number of different guardianship agreements. The principal must have procedures in place to guarantee the correct adult takes a child from school or receives a progress report.

Security is no longer a minor issue. Use this meeting to review every aspect of your security plan. Remember to involve teachers because staff members frequently take shortcuts to their cars and leave building doors, once thought to be secured, open. A principal from Maine stated that her building was compromised by an aide who left a rock in the base of a panic door so that she could come and go by the rear exit. (See Resource 9: Building Security Memo.)

Personal Commentary/Notes: _____

_____

* Oversee Orientation of New Students

The principal should meet with all new students. One middle school principal from Long Island, New York, has lunch with all new students during the second week of school. He then has them come to his office and asks them about the first few days of school. This is a good way to review the school's registration procedures. The same middle school principal asks each team to give him a note about each new student's adjustment to classes. In this case, the follow up might best be handled by the student's counselor.

Personal Commentary/Notes: _____

_____

Meet With New Teachers *

The orientation process should be ongoing throughout the year. We detailed the many aspects of the program in August Key Tasks. We urge that the principal meet with the new teachers during the first day to review every topic that is necessary for the school opening. Although this can be delegated to a supervisor or mentor, the checklist should be provided by the principal.

By now there should be a specific orientation agenda for the school year. Items such as classroom discipline, lesson planning, grading procedures, and techniques for meeting with parents should be high priorities. (See Resource 10: Principal's Orientation Presentation.)

Personal Commentary/Notes: _____

_____

Initiate Staff Development Plans *

Have each department create a staff development plan for the year, which should be linked to building and district goals. These plans provide a framework for distributing funds and resources for staff development and help the principal set up priorities for staff attendance at conferences and training programs. Most important, it makes faculty members aware of the principal's expectation—that we are forever, and above all else, teachers and learners.

Personal Commentary/Notes: _____

_____

Establish the Disciplinary Process *

Due to an ever-increasing number of legal challenges, many states have enacted laws requiring school districts to have written disciplinary codes. These plans are quite comprehensive and include the recommended punishment and remediation prescribed for a variety of infractions. They limit the authority of the school principal so that any action taken is more defensible in a court of law.

Instead of attempting to adjust our philosophy to every state law, what follows is a disciplinary tool that is based on the concepts of process and progression. The process ensures that the student receives a fair handling for each infraction, while at the same time, the progression allows for a stricter remediation if the child is a repeat offender. Unlike the criminal justice system, school principals do take into consideration all previous infractions when taking action on repeat offenders.

We endorse a referral form that incorporates the following disciplinary components:

1. Precise record keeping is required of every offense for every student.

2. Teachers must give a factual description of the incident. The use of psychological jargon is discouraged—for example, "Billy hit John and was not provoked in any manner," rather than "Billy is showing aggressive tendencies and inner hostility."

3. The teacher should describe the child's past behavior. For example, "Billy on several occasions has pulled chairs out from under students and struck smaller classmates."

4. The teacher should describe previous attempts to resolve the problem. For example, the teacher might write, "I have talked with Billy, kept him after class, have called his parents, and have met with his mother."

5. The principal should describe any action taken. Putting the principal's decision in writing and giving a copy to the teacher serves as a direct communication to the teacher who made the referral. Most collaborative principals suggest that teachers come in to discuss the action taken if they are not satisfied with how the administrator handled the infraction.

6. A second copy of this report goes to other administrators involved in handling disciplinary cases. This guarantees that everyone is informed and aware of all student problems.

7. A third copy goes to the student's counselor, who is expected to discuss the matter with the student. We agree that counselors should not be disciplinarians, but they should be involved in the process. They are experts in exploring with the student alternative behaviors and helping students to ascertain why they behaved in such a manner.

8. The fourth copy goes back to the teacher as stated in Step 5 of this process.

The proper filing of these forms maintains an accurate history of every infraction and gives evidence that as the incidents increased, so too did the disciplinary progression. Nothing was done in an arbitrary manner, and, in fact, the goal of the principal, teacher, and counselor was to modify the child's behavior and improve his or her conduct in school.

Finally, remember that the best teacher, curriculum, and facilities do not guarantee educational excellence. The essential additional ingredient needed to maximize student learning is an outstanding disciplinary tone.

Personal Commentary/Notes: _____

_____

Middle-level educators have long recognized the need for a comprehensive guidance program. This involves trained guidance counselors and a teacher-based advisory program. The teachers and counselors complement each other as they attempt to address the needs of early adolescents. Guidance counselors should be the student-centered conscience of the staff. They should be deeply involved in monitoring student progress. Parents should be contacted whenever a counselor or staff member observes a change in behavior. For the most part, the counselor or social worker is the liaison between the school and the home.

We should inform staff members about the functions of the guidance department and the expectations we have for teachers to augment the efforts of counselors. The extended guidance program is spelled out in the following National Association of Secondary School Principals (NASSP) article:

Personal Commentary/Notes: _____

_____

Essential Elements of an Extended Guidance Program

1. Caring adults must be present as role models for the students.

2. If possible, a consistent peer group should meet regularly.

3. Community service projects should involve students as individuals and in groups.

4. Student decision making should be encouraged and taught.

5. A CARE (Concerned About Reaching Everyone) team should be established.

6. A wellness program for students and teachers should be provided.

7. Age-appropriate social activities should be provided.

8. At-risk students should be identified early.

9. All students should be surveyed often.

10. The guidance curriculum should be based on student needs.

SOURCE: Bergmann, S. (1991). Guidance in the middle level school: The compassion component. In J. Capelluti & D. Stokes (Ed.), *Middle level education programs, policies, and practices.* Reston, VA: National Association of Secondary School Principals.

✳ *Establish an Advisory Program*

Most middle schools schedule an advisory period a few days each week, although sometimes it is simply an extended homeroom period. The purpose of an advisory program is to allow students to get to know an additional adult in the building and be able to discuss personal matters within a small group. Some schools divide the number of students by every professional staff member in the building to keep the groups very small. Still others have adopted formal mini-lessons based on the needs of the group.

In Half Hollow Hills on Long Island in New York, there are two middle schools. Both principals have their own advisory groups. They also keep the same students for three years. This is indicative of a truly hands-on principal.

Personal Commentary/Notes: _____

_____

✳ *Complete Superintendent Reports*

Remember to complete all necessary school reports. Your secretary should have due date reminders on your desk the week before the reports are due. Additionally, send the superintendent items you would like to have announced at board of education meetings. Share with the superintendent good news about your students, faculty, or school.

Personal Commentary/Notes: _____

_____

✳ *Provide Orientation for Public Address System Users*

Meet with all staff and students who regularly use the public address system to review expectations, limits, and the appropriateness of announcements. A major goal should be to limit the use of the public address system to homeroom announcements. Using it during the day is a serious violation of your academic tone and a major complaint of classroom teachers.

Personal Commentary/Notes: _____

_____

✳ *Meet With Extracurricular Advisors*

The extracurricular program of activities and clubs is a vital part of the middle school philosophy. Meet with all advisors to review procedures and to schedule activities to avoid conflicts. Wherever possible, we want students to be involved and not be forced to choose one activity over another. Few middle schools have guidebooks for these activities and membership requirements, which would help standardize procedures and advertise the program.

Personal Commentary/Notes: _____

_____

Conduct Required Safety Drills *

As stated under the section about security plans, no topic is more important than ensuring the safety of your children and staff. At a minimum, follow the mandates of your state and local requirements. As mentioned before, it's essential to have a preannounced fire drill, followed a day or two later by an unannounced drill. This should be done no later than the second week of school.

Many principals go on the public address system to discuss the seriousness of fire drills. Remember our quote from the fire department, "If the building isn't exited in under two minutes, there is a strong possibility of fatalities." Praising the children after the first preannounced drill is a positive affirmation of their behavior.

Personal Commentary/Notes: _____

_____

Begin Student Spirit Activities *

Teachers should discuss schoolwide activities that motivate children to become involved. Decorated bulletin board displays and welcome-to-school signs set a good tone. Publicizing the first major school event serves as a reminder that middle schools can also be fun. Student council activities should also be advertised, along with the election of sixth grade officers. We assume the present seventh and eighth graders had their election in the spring of the previous year.

Personal Commentary/Notes: _____

_____

Complete Annual Grant Proposals *

Work with the appropriate central office and building staff to identify and complete all required grant proposals and take advantage of some of the many optional grants that are available. Grant funds can serve as a significant supplement to the budget and can provide funding for those last-minute opportunities for special programs and activities that would otherwise not be affordable.

Remember, small grants are sometimes available from your local service organizations, such as the Lions Club, Rotary Club, and the Elks Club.

Personal Commentary/Notes: _____

_____

September Communications

* Compose Weekly Memo to Staff

A weekly memo to staff organizes the entire school community. The purpose of the correspondence is to remind everyone about the events of the week, future activities, and due dates. Middle school faculties are larger than elementary school faculties, and thus it's difficult for the principal to have daily contact with each teacher. The weekly memo helps to bridge that gap.

Teachers and teams should be encouraged to submit items to make the memo a two-way correspondence. A section devoted to future events helps to avoid conflicts. (See Resource 11: Principal's Weekly Bulletin.)

Personal Commentary/Notes: _____

_____

* Meet With Each Teacher Team

As it is with the subject departments, teams should have goals for the year. The first meeting should include the team's guidance counselor, so the team can have a brief discussion about children who are having adjustment problems. Team activities should be planned, so items such as field trips can be added to the principal's weekly memo under the heading of future events.

Personal Commentary/Notes: _____

_____

* Report to PTA, Superintendent, and Board of Education on School Opening

As the most visible spokesperson for your school, issuing both oral and written reports to the major constituencies you serve is important. Use the first PTA and board of education meetings of the school year to highlight the opening of the building. You may wish to focus on the many positive faculty accomplishments completed over the summer and the smooth manner in which instruction began.

A description of the adjustment of the new incoming class usually adds a poignant touch.

Personal Commentary/Notes: _____

_____

Meet With School Improvement ∗
Teams and Site-Based Councils

Most states have requirements for the participation of staff, parents, and, sometimes, students in the school decision-making process. The format may vary from district to district. Some councils are extremely effective, whereas others discuss banalities such as where to put flowerpots.

September is the time to meet with these groups to discuss plans and activities for the coming year, formalize meeting schedules and procedures, and set goals for the year. Sharing building ownership with key constituent groups contributes to a positive school climate and enhances the principal's ability to address critical issues. If one truthfully believes in parental and staff involvement, the site-based teams should become strong allies in the middle school improvement process. (See Resource 12: Effective Teamwork and Group Leadership.)

Personal Commentary/Notes: _____

_____

Meet With School Nurse(s) ∗

Many principals do not have the services of a nurse or school nurse teacher. When a nurse is not available, the tasks we discuss in this section must be delegated or performed by the principal. Our nurse must inform teachers about every health deficiency of the students in their charge. Accommodations passed by the committee on special education should also be communicated to the staff. We make this a dual responsibility of the nurse and the chairperson of the child study team (CST). When we use the term *staff*, we want it to apply to every employee who comes in contact with a child.

Nurses should maintain emergency home contact cards in the event a child needs to be sent home from school. The nurse calls the home or place of business to inform the parent of the child's need to go home. Many nurses are very involved in drug education programs, first aid instruction, and the use of a defibrillator.

The nurse also analyzes illness trends. Calls to the principal will alert school leaders about hair lice, skin infections, flu epidemics, and other health emergencies. In the event of food poisoning, the nurse's office may be inundated by sick children. Plans should be developed to deal with such emergencies. The nurse also serves as a health counselor to children, parents, and staff members.

Personal Commentary/Notes: _____

_____

* Write and Distribute Memo Regarding Special Education Accommodations

It is the Committee on Special Education's responsibility to meet and discuss each special education child's program. Both classified and 504 students are entitled by law to a variety of accommodations. The principal must ensure that the faculty has been informed about every accommodation. Teachers must be provided with a list of students in each category and the assistance they are entitled to receive. All memos related to special education matters should be clearly marked "confidential" to protect student privacy. (See Resource 13: Best Practices in Quality Education for Students With Severe Disabilities.)

Personal Commentary/Notes: _____

_____

* Conduct Class Visits

We touch base with every staff member by making a quick visit to each classroom during the first few days of school. With new teachers, the principal may want to simply prepare the staff member for his or her frequent drop-in visits. Many principals talk to the class for a moment about the school's expectations and student behavior. The physical presence of the principal lets everyone know that he or she is a hands-on administrator. Management by walking around (MBWA) is a valid practice for middle school administrators.

Personal Commentary/Notes: _____

_____

* Send Open School Night Invitation to All Parents

A personal letter sent to every parent or guardian inviting them to Open School Night is a necessity in September. The letter should include the agenda for the evening, a description of expectations, and a reminder to parents that the focus is on the curriculum, not parent-teacher conferences. A meeting will be held later in the year for the latter purpose.

Provide refreshments in the cafeteria and invite students to serve as hosts. The children should also serve as guides to enable parents to find each classroom. PTA members should be stationed throughout the building or in the cafeteria to collect membership applications. The PTA can also advertise their first meeting and distribute handouts listing all future meeting dates.

Personal Commentary/Notes: _____

_____

Write Article for Principal's Newsletter to Parents *****

A monthly letter home from the principal is an opportunity to share staff awards and to inform parents about pressing issues. A calendar of important school dates and events should be included, similar to what is given to staff in the weekly memo. Information on team accomplishments and plans for the future helps to create an air of anticipation. Routines should also be spelled out for parents. Some examples of information to be shared include procedures for absence notes, early dismissals, security measures, and testing dates, as well as the role of guidance. The latter is imperative since many elementary schools do not have guidance counselors.

Personal Commentary/Notes: _____

_____

September Planning

Develop Assembly *****
Procedures and Plans

September is a wonderful time to build school spirit, share important information, and support the curriculum of classroom teachers. Just as we recommended for the first fire drill, great attention should be paid to organizing the first assembly. Describing the role of each teacher at a faculty meeting is worthwhile. Perhaps the following suggestions seem to be overkill, but they are offered because failure is not an option in such gatherings:

1. Turn off the bells, particularly if it's a grade-level assembly.

2. Discuss entrance into the auditorium.

3. Check the public address system in the auditorium prior to the start of the assembly.

4. Determine who will bring the assembly to order.

5. Discuss how teachers will assist in quieting classes.

6. Provide a seating chart for classes.

7. Have teachers instruct students in every class about appropriate assembly behavior.

8. Discuss the proper method of exiting an assembly.

9. Decide which subject department will follow up on the content of the program.

10. Prepare a formal announcement to indicate the resumption of classes and possible changes in the bell schedule following an assembly.

Personal Commentary/Notes: _____

_____

* *Prepare for Open School Night*

Even though letters of invitation have been written to parents, our staff must be organized for the event. We need a secretary to have backup student schedules for parents who arrive without them. As mentioned before, student guides should also be available to direct parents to their child's classrooms. Arrange for refreshments with the PTA, the cafeteria staff, or both.

Hosting a mini-assembly to start the evening allows the principal to introduce key staff members. Many administrators offer copies of the first principal newsletter to parents. The principal may even call for volunteers to serve on committees, such as site-based teams. The entire session should not exceed fifteen minutes, but the warmth of the welcome should last all evening. (See Resource 14: Open School Night Memo to Teachers.)

Personal Commentary/Notes: _____

_____

* *Develop Guidance Newsletters*

Maintaining regular communication with parents is vitally important for middle schoolers. Some type of guidance newsletter should go home several times a year. A canned one may be used at the beginning of the year to explain guidance services, especially for new sixth graders. Articles submitted by staff members, departments, and teams are welcomed.

Hot topics of the day should be handled in an informational format. In the past few years, we've had to deal with AIDS, pornographic materials, illegal drug use, and security fears, as well as the usual adolescent topics of dating, responsibilities versus rights, bullying, friendships, and relationships with peers. The newsletter should include a question-and-answer column so that students and parents can participate.

Personal Commentary/Notes: _____

_____

Make Plans for an Evening Event *
With Coaches and Advisors

Principals who host an evening event to meet with coaches and advisors report a large attendance by parents and children. This is truly a middle school activity in which students are given the opportunity to learn new skills and try out different activities.

For superior athletes, coaches may attend and discuss tryouts, practices, and time requirements. This last element is important since the involved student has to manage his or her time in an efficient manner to ensure that schoolwork will not suffer.

In this high-tech era, videos of games and activities from the previous year should serve as a motivational tool. Opportunities for parents to become members of booster clubs help make their involvement a reality.

Personal Commentary/Notes: _____

Plan Schoolwide Staff Development Activities *

Most districts provide for conference days in their school calendar. These sessions are used to relay curriculum information, state mandates, and new legal requirements to teachers. In the past few years, teachers have had to attend seminars to become aware of child abuse legislation, HIV disease, sexual harassment policies, state curriculum standards, security procedures, and right-to-know laws.

Conference should meet the district's needs, but teacher concerns should be addressed as well. This is an excellent topic for site-based teams or for a separate conference day committee. Some administrators continue to define shared decision making as "I'll make the decision and then share it with the staff." Middle school principals have embraced the true meaning of shared decision making. This conference affords principals a perfect opportunity to practice what they advocate.

Personal Commentary/Notes: _____

Maintain and Review Student Activities Calendar *

With the enormous number of middle school events, a schoolwide calendar should be displayed in the principal's office. Every event should be listed to avoid conflicts with other organizations or important school activities. The school secretary should be the only person to list activities, and this should not be done unless she receives a note from the principal to do so. This may sound rigid, but we have found that it's the only way to avoid conflicts and hurt feelings. Principals can list events in this calendar the same way they list future events on the weekly memo to staff. Before the year begins, holidays, testing dates, report card dates, interim reporting times, and faculty meetings can be posted. It is, in fact, a living calendar.

Personal Commentary/Notes: _____

_____

* *Monitor Field Trip Requests*

No one will debate the value of field trips if they are to quality places and if they reinforce the grade level's curriculum. We have found that too often the field trip merely serves as a day off from school. To ensure these excursions are valuable, here are some suggestions:

1. Make a list with your staff of quality places to host middle school children.

2. Annual trips to the same local places by all grade levels diminish the value of the experience.

3. Have teachers submit several objectives prior to approving the trip.

4. Give priority approval to those that are tied to valuable objectives and to the grade's curriculum.

5. Guard against teachers who abuse the educational value of field experiences by scheduling a countless number of trips.

Personal Commentary/Notes: _____

_____

September Personnel

* *Distribute Emergency Information*

Have your emergency plans ready; don't wait for cold weather or a sudden disaster to force you to devise them. Your secretary should update and distribute to every staff member the emergency phone chain at the start of school. In the case of an emergency, one call to the class mother activates the chain, and all parents in the chain are called and informed about the emergency. The chain is a valuable tool to use in weather emergencies or when a personal or schoolwide crisis occurs. Emergency chains for parents should also be done for each class. This is an excellent activity for PTA leaders, who assign a class mother or two to each homeroom to coordinate the information.

Personal Commentary/Notes: _____

_____

Meet With Faculty Sunshine Committee *

The principal is the symbolic leader of the school, which, we hope, is thought of as a family. As in any family, key events should be acknowledged. The principal should work closely with the sunshine committee to send cards when a pleasurable event occurs. Perhaps more important, the committee expresses condolences and regrets when a staff member suffers a personal loss. Keep a supply of sympathy, get-well, thank-you, congratulatory, and birthday cards on hand.

Personal Commentary/Notes: _____

_____

Develop a School Directory *

Creating and distributing a school directory to parents and students is a service that your community will appreciate. The directory should include important school district and community phone numbers as well as a list of students by grade with their addresses and phone numbers. Be sure to give families the right to opt out of the directory for privacy concerns.

Personal Commentary/Notes: _____

_____

Mail Faculty Start-of-School Materials *

One way to avoid an opening faculty meeting that merely reviews all of the little details is to mail faculty their handbooks and special memos a week before school begins. Although not all faculty members will read these in advance, many of your staff will appreciate this opportunity, which allows them to concentrate on getting their rooms and materials ready, rather than sitting in a long and sometimes boring opening meeting. It also provides an opportunity for teachers who have read the material to raise questions and offer suggestions.

Personal Commentary/Notes: _____

_____

* *Set Up Schedule Changes Week With Guidance Department*

The week before school starts is often the busiest and most hectic of the year. Providing an additional week or two for the guidance staff to come in before classes start ensures a smooth start to the school year. During this week, counselors can make schedule changes for students who attended summer school, students new to the community, or students who simply want to change their class schedule. Working out schedule changes early prevents unnecessary confusion after the start of school.

Personal Commentary/Notes: _____

_____

* *Schedule Teacher Observations and Evaluations*

Evaluation of the teaching staff is one of the most important responsibilities of the principal. Develop a plan to ensure that all district and state deadlines for teacher observations and evaluations are met. Meet with department chairpersons, supervisors, and assistant principals to review the format and process for evaluating teachers. All too often, teacher incompetence hearings are lost because of a mistake made in the process. Careful planning will avoid this and focus attention on the real issue—the quality of teaching in the classroom.

If the middle school principal held meaningful final evaluations in June, the goals for the new school year should be developed. Plan as intensely for your finest staff members as you do for your new or weaker teachers. The excellent teacher needs to be motivated and perhaps given greater responsibilities.

Personal Commentary/Notes: _____

_____

* *Review Administrative Team Objectives*

Each member of the principal's administrative team should be expected to develop objectives or goals for the year. Many of us work alone, but we may have curriculum directors to assist us. The principal should provide direction for the creation of yearly objectives and meet individually with each person to approve the objectives. An end-of-year meeting to assess progress in meeting these objectives or goals should be a regular part of the evaluation process.

Many of us do not receive the assistance we need from supervisors stationed in the secondary schools. Middle school principals must be assertive and demand equal time for their building and curriculum needs.

Personal Commentary/Notes: _____

_____

September Checklists

September Key Tasks

Major Assignments	Date Started	Date Completed	Days on Task
Conduct first faculty meeting			
Review opening preparations			
Meet with staff to discuss security plans			
Oversee orientation of new students			
Meet with new teachers			
Initiate staff development plans			
Establish the disciplinary process			
Review guidance program's direction			
Establish an advisory program			
Complete superintendent reports			
Provide orientation for public address system users			
Meet with extracurricular advisors			
Conduct required safety drills			
Begin student spirit activities			
Complete annual grant proposals			

September Communications

✓	Assignment
	Compose weekly memo to staff
	Meet with each teacher team
	Report to PTA, superintendent, and board of education on school opening
	Meet with school improvement teams and site-based councils
	Meet with school nurse(s)
	Write and distribute memo regarding special education accommodations
	Conduct class visits
	Send Open School Night invitation to all parents
	Write article for principal's newsletter to parents

September Planning

✓	Assignment
	Develop assembly procedures and plans
	Prepare for Open School Night
	Develop guidance newsletters
	Make plans for an evening event with coaches and advisors
	Plan schoolwide staff development activities
	Maintain and review student activities calendar
	Monitor field trip requests

September Personnel

✓	Finalize
	Distribute emergency information
	Meet with faculty sunshine committee
	Develop a school directory
	Mail faculty start-of-school materials
	Set up schedule changes week with guidance department
	Schedule teacher observations and evaluations
	Review administrative team objectives

September Calendar

MONTH: SEPTEMBER

YEAR: _____

MONDAY	TUESDAY	WEDNESDAY	THURSDAY	FRIDAY	SATURDAY
					SUNDAY
					SATURDAY
					SUNDAY
					SATURDAY
					SUNDAY
					SATURDAY
					SUNDAY
					SATURDAY
					SUNDAY

NOTES _____

Chapter Four

Words to live by are just words, unless we live by them.

—Eric Harvey and Alexander Lucia

*I*f school opened smoothly in September, our passion for excellence and dedication to detail were amply rewarded. There are those who exhale in relief and believe that October will be a lull before the increased tempo of the November and December holiday excitement. We strongly differ. The pace you have set must be maintained and your planning accelerated to harness the energy needed to meet your high expectations for the entire first semester.

Oliver Wendell Holmes said, "I find the important thing in life is not where we are, but in what direction we are moving." In October, your faculty and students have probably settled into established routines. Just looking at this month's key tasks should be enough to help principals focus on the challenges ahead. In doing so, principals also energize their faculty by making them aware of the four key areas of October.

First, there is the beginning of the following year's budget process. No, it's not too early to start analyzing your building's needs. You may wish to start with items that were not included from your past wish list. Second, interim reports of student progress need to be sent home. These, as we later show, inform family members about their children's academic progress and behavior in school. Third, creative planning is needed for Halloween. Responsible principals believe that developing constructive activities around Halloween helps to eliminate the potential for destructive incidents. The final key task is to intensify the new teacher orientation program. Remember that every item in the orientation for new teachers should serve as a review for your experienced staff members. In addition to assisting new teachers with their own professional development and classroom techniques, we feel an obligation to have them understand the purpose of middle school education. An effective middle school has the following characteristics:

1. Has a program that responds to the physical, intellectual, and social needs of adolescents

2. Has a mission statement that guides the staff and the program

3. Helps to prepare students for the high school's academic and social challenges

4. Organizes instruction with teams of teachers, so they can collaborate on instructional goals and recognize, use, and capitalize on children's individual characteristics

5. Ensures that every student has one or more adults to confide in and to nurture their development

6. Never loses sight of the necessity for a strong academic curriculum, which goes hand in hand with concern for children

7. Offers opportunity for exploration and for children to learn their strengths and weaknesses

8. Offers a team structure and flexible time periods for instruction, based on the needs of children

9. Periodically evaluates programs and activities, either by staff or outside consultants, to enhance learning and expand student opportunities

10. Employs teachers who enjoy the age group, work collaboratively with colleagues, and understand the value of a comprehensive guidance program

These characteristics are shared with staff at faculty meetings and in the new teacher orientation program. When speaking about certain educational experiences, the principal should remind the faculty that so many of the things we do are consistent with these areas.

We are attempting to develop a staff committed to our students. Dr. Howard Johnson, in answer to the question "What makes a good teacher?" received a heartwarming response from those in attendance at a middle school conference: "A teacher who is approachable, has a sense of humor, cares about students, is willing to stay after school and help, participates in student activities, and is encouraging." For principals who want to develop this kind of faculty, October is not a time to coast. Remember, if you coast, you can only go downhill.

October Key Tasks

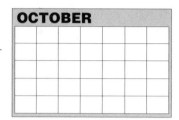

* *Set Budget Development Timelines and Parameters*

The budget process presents logical opportunities for staff involvement. No topic is open to greater participation than the budgetary process. Principals recently conducted a walk-through with the head custodian, and reconvening a meeting with the custodian is the first step in drafting the budget wish list. Major capital expenditures are usually items that are in long-range plans for the school plant. New boilers, roofs, windows, and floors are major budgetary expenditures. Principals find that these items are often eliminated when the first request is made. Revisiting these facility improvements every year ensures that the superintendent and board of education are aware of your perceived needs. Sometimes, what you don't get initially will be budgeted a year or two later. Unfortunately, when budgets come in higher than expected, the first items eliminated are large capital expenditures.

We concentrate on building maintenance and repair early in the year. Later in the school year, the teaching staff is requested to give their input about their instructional space. Painting, new furniture, file cabinets, maps, and other in-room improvements are the initial requests of the teachers. In future months, we request from the teaching and supervisory staff their curriculum needs. Textbooks, curriculum-writing projects, summer school items, and new technology await updated state education requirements. The need for disposable items is determined by the use and abuse of such material during the school year. In the resource section, we include a school district's budget calendar to give a fuller view of the month-by-month opportunity to plan and to involve one's staff. (See Resource 15: Budget Process Calendar.)

Personal Commentary/Notes: _____

_____

* *Review Interim Reports*

Last month, we reviewed with staff all the written comments that they might use on interim reports. We do this because needs change as time passes, and also some departments require unique comments. For example, technology teachers may want to comment on manual dexterity, whereas the foreign language department may want a comment dealing with pronunciation. This is consistent with the middle school philosophy, which states we should frequently reevaluate our goals and techniques.

Interim reports ensure that parents are aware of their child's progress. The reports also perform the following functions:

- Guarantee that changes in student performance are communicated
- Prompt counselors to discuss progress with their students
- Let administrators know about multiple failures and students who are misbehaving in class
- Allow department chairs to focus on new teachers who may be experiencing disciplinary problems
- Alert team teachers concerning students who are having difficulty in other classes and enable the teachers to offer assistance to colleagues
- Allow teachers to commend students who are performing well, exhibiting good citizenship, or showing exceptional effort

The complementary interim report should not be minimized. Frequently, positive comments often encourage the continuance of good behavior and help foster students' drive for academic excellence. This is consistent with several goals of our middle school philosophy. The interim report helps students to learn their strengths and weaknesses and gives evidence of how the staff nurtures each child.

In this age of foreign-born immigrants, who may speak a language other than English, many districts have written interim reports in Spanish, Portuguese, or other languages. It shows a great deal of sensitivity to translate interim reports into home languages, even though our primary goal seeks to enable everyone to communicate in English. (See Resource 16: Interim Progress Reports Memo.)

Personal Commentary/Notes: _____

_____

Prepare for Open School Night ✳

We've already stressed the importance of hosting an Open House. Sending invitations to parents is a wonderful way to show that their participation would be welcomed. Careful planning is critical to the success of the evening. Be sure the school has a pleasant appearance, extra student schedules are available, and refreshments are provided in the cafeteria. Have students from one of your service groups act as guides to help parents find their way to their child's class and to other key areas in the building.

Ideally, it would be beneficial to have a parent night in September to discuss grade-level requirements, homework expectations, the purposes of teaming, and means to improve parent-teacher communication. The second meeting in October or November should be to talk with parents or guardians about the progress and behavior of individual students. Some teacher contracts may limit the number of evening meetings. Half-day school conferences have been used, but in an era of working parents, these are at times problematic. Day and evening conferences are obviously ideal for reaching out to busy parents.

Principals should not take it for granted that every teacher is prepared to conduct a professional conference with parents. Discussions at faculty meetings, role-playing exercises, and a memorandum to staff should provide the necessary advice and guidance. This should definitely be a part of your new teacher orientation program.

Personal Commentary/Notes: _____

_____

* *Plan Halloween Dance and Alternative Activities*

Channeling the middle school age group's enormous energy is particularly helpful during holidays. Halloween is often associated with negative behavior and violence. Work with your PTA and student government officers to plan positive activities. Using middle school children to provide a carnival for elementary students is a way for the older students to set a good example for the K–5 students. Booths with games are set up, and the PTA furnishes prizes for winners of each activity. Children who come to the carnival sign pledges that they will not go trick-or-treating at night.

Principals and middle school staff members should find ways to change a holiday associated with vandalism and violence into one associated with more wholesome activities. This is also a topic that can be discussed at team and faculty meetings. One team in New York uses the holiday to kick off their Thanksgiving Day food drive. Those children who go trick-or-treating collect food for the needy. This is publicized as part of the school's public relations (PR) program. What a wonderful way to change a negative possibility into a positive achievement.

Personal Commentary/Notes: _____

_____

* *Screen New Entrants*

Although this is an ongoing process throughout the year, late admissions to your school should be properly screened. We train our secretary and school nurse in these procedures, but like so many other things, it is ultimately the principal's responsibility. We offer the following recommendations:

1. Evidence of state health requirements, such as vaccinations, must be presented prior to admission to school.

2. Residency documents, such as rent receipts, telephone bills, or tax receipts, must be verified to allow children to be educated in your district.

3. A secretary should be trained to verify residency and health documents prior to the student meeting with the academic screening committee or counselors.

4. Evaluate the student's background and provide a system for this information to be given to the classroom teacher when appropriate.

5. Make sure immediate action is taken if the new student is in need of special services.

6. Have the counselor make the best possible team placement for each student.

7. Make a concerted effort to obtain records from the student's previous schools.

Personal Commentary/Notes: _____

Review Progress of Students in Need of Special Services *

This is your guarantee that no student slips through the cracks in your school. It also keeps you aware of trends in your own student body. Principals should know the number of children receiving services in categories such as second languages, resource room, speech, and special education. Regular meetings with special education staff members should help to keep the principal informed about each child's IEP (Individual Educational Program). On the surface, this sounds like an awesome responsibility, especially in a large school, but organized principals keep an annotated file for each child receiving services. When meeting with a parent, principals can glance at the material, thus giving the parent a feeling of confidence in the school's staff.

There also should be regularly scheduled meetings with the leaders of the Committee on Special Education. If the school has a SEPTA (Special Education Parent-Teacher Association), attendance at these meetings is recommended. If the principal is not present, make certain another administrator or liaison to the organization is in attendance.

Principals should include methods for meeting the needs of special education students at faculty meetings and in new teacher orientation. (See Resource 17: Attention-Deficit Disorders.)

Personal Commentary/Notes: _____

Review Plans for Faculty Meetings *

Faculty meetings are often lost opportunities for relevant inservice training and morale boosting. Several principals reported to us that they formed a faculty agenda committee, whose purpose is to develop the content for each meeting. The session becomes a collaboratively planned session. The principal does not give up his or her authority but receives information about faculty concerns and perceptions about their needs from these committee members. Many useful topics come from this form of joint planning.

Personal Commentary/Notes: _____

_____

* *Hold First Site-Based Committee Meeting*

After making sure that new members to the site-based team receive inservice training concerning the decision-making process, the first meeting should be called. A typical agenda includes the following:

1. A review of last year's accomplishments and unfinished topics

2. Selection of a new facilitator

3. Exploration of new topics for the year and designing procedures for reviewing ideas received from the entire staff

4. Maintenance of a timetable for the meetings, since everyone has other responsibilities, which prevents the meeting taking a rambling, show-and-tell format

Personal Commentary/Notes: _____

_____

* *Coordinate the Year's Testing Program*

Work with the faculty to develop a comprehensive testing program for your students, since there are both district and state testing requirements. Make certain that you put yourself in your students' shoes and develop a sensible date for each examination. Spread the test dates throughout the year so that children are not overwhelmed and testing does not interfere with major school events, holidays, and other testing periods. Some states are mandating a host of assessments for middle school students. In New York, as many as seven examinations have been required for middle school students. This is certainly overkill in the recent quest for accountability. Middle school principals are urged to stand up for the many other intangibles involved in the instructional process, such as taking time for the teachable moment and inculcating an enthusiasm for learning.

Additionally, principals should allow teachers to prepare children for the test and its format, but not all instruction should be geared toward the exam. If principals put great pressure on their staff during testing periods, you can be sure this anxiety will be transmitted to students. Ideally, tests should provide necessary feedback regarding the thoroughness of our instructional program. The principal should include methods for meeting the needs of special education students, which are identified through testing, at faculty meetings and during new teacher orientation.

Tests should not be viewed as the sole indicator of the success of a school. Unfortunately, in this era of rigid standards, principals are in the unique position of attempting to maximize test results while maintaining enthusiasm for the teaching process and the caring classroom environment. This position is made even more untenable if test scores are viewed by the superintendent and the community as the school's only indicator of success.

Personal Commentary/Notes: _____

_____

Initiate Grade-Level Plans *

Much attention is given to the adjustment of the incoming sixth graders. Even though their assimilation into the middle school remains a priority for the entire staff, special events should also be planned for our remaining two grades. These activities might include fundraising drives for worthy causes, class and team trips, class photographs, concerts, yearbooks, and moving up exercises. Meeting with class officers and their advisors to set the priorities and dates for the year's events is recommended. It is also another opportunity to stress behavioral expectations for such activities.

As principals, we not only want to ensure the development of wholesome activities geared to this age group, but we also want to create a conflict-free calendar. Planning an all-day activity followed by a formal testing day is inexcusable. When things run smoothly, it is never a result of casual planning.

Personal Commentary/Notes: _____

_____

Plan Homecoming Parade and Activities *

Most high schools celebrate a homecoming event, which often includes a parade and other festivities. Middle school children should be represented. If there is a parade, we recommend that every middle school club and organization become active participants. As soon as the theme is selected, the principal should solicit staff, students, and parents to construct a float and encourage participants to march in the parade. Monitor the plans for homecoming for safety and provide appropriate supervision for those participating. Sending a letter home to parents will help maximize audience participation.

Personal Commentary/Notes: _____

_____

* Coordinate Recognition Day With Board of Education

Remember to communicate your goals and the staff's accomplishments to the board of education and the superintendent. Recognize honors received by children at these times; showcase their talents, interests, and service to the community.

Invite board members to visit the school, and send personal invitations to each trustee to all of your school's major events. After attending your activities, most board members report the visit during board of education meetings. They, in a sense, become your PR representatives to the community. This often has a far-reaching, spiraling effect since local newspaper reporters covering the board meeting frequently make mention of the event in their subsequent articles.

Personal Commentary/Notes: _____

_____

* Conduct Fire and Emergency Drills

If you're located in a cold winter region, conduct your fire drills early in the school year. Maintain a good relationship with the local fire department since they provide many additional services. We have fire personnel visit our health classes to discuss CPR training, fire safety training, and training in the use of defibrillators.

Many superintendents must notify the state education department indicating compliance with the required number of drills. Some districts require emergency go-home drills. Principals should send a note to the central office after each drill and after all the drills have been conducted.

Personal Commentary/Notes: _____

_____

October Communications

* Plan Monthly Board of Education Presentation

In addition to the items discussed under this month's key tasks, serious attention should be paid to preparing a middle school board presentation. Highlight programs the community should know about, and work with appropriate staff members to prepare the format and presentation. If children are able to participate, it will be better received.

In this way, the board and community will become more knowledgeable about the topics you present and thus more supportive for your program's goals. Again, the local press will take pictures of your students making a presentation, and this adds to the school's reputation. Showcasing children isn't a shameless PR campaign but an advertisement of their success and the success of the staff.

Personal Commentary/Notes: _____

_____

Help Plan Monthly PTA Meetings *

Principals should never miss a PTA meeting. Take an active role in helping parents plan their programs. Try to motivate staff to truly become the *T* in PTA. Invite them to attend a meeting to report on aspects of programs, student achievements, and team activities. Obviously, we believe the principal should report at every PTA meeting about major events and issues of interest to parents.

Strategies for improving parental involvement are detailed here, as they appeared in the brochure *Schools in the Middle* (National Association of Secondary School Principals, n.d.).

Strategies for Parent/Family Involvement

The September 1991 *ERIC Review,* published by the U.S. Department of Education's Office of Educational Research and Improvement, identified the following strategies to encourage parent involvement, especially single and working parents, non-English-speaking parents, and poor and minority parents.

- Increase the awareness and sensitivity of school staff members to parents' time constraints; announce meetings enough in advance to allow parents to plan to attend.
- Give parents blanket permission to visit the school at any time to visit the classroom, use the library, or talk to the teachers and administrators.
- Establish or support family learning centers in schools, storefronts, and churches, and offer help to parents who want to help their children learn.
- Make the school facilities available to a variety of community activities.
- Facilitate teen, single, working, and custodial-parent peer support groups.

- Provide before-school child care so working parents can see teachers before going to work.
- Conduct evening meetings with child care so working parents can attend.
- Conduct evening awards assemblies to recognize students and parents for their contributions to the school.
- Establish bilingual hotlines for parents.
- Send bilingual messages to parents not only with regard to routine information but also regarding things parents can do at home to help educate their children.
- Do not make last-minute school cancellations.
- Print all signs in the school in the languages spoken by school families.

Personal Commentary/Notes: _____

_____

* Schedule K–12 Principals' Meetings

The middle school principal should meet monthly with the high school and elementary school principals. This helps promote articulation and allows an opportunity to make any necessary curriculum revisions as changes are made at different levels. We believe it's counterproductive and destructive for any principal to denigrate another school's work. This belief should be passed on to the entire staff. It is evident that the middle school can learn much from their K–5 and 9–12 colleagues.

Remember that many of your staff members are part of districtwide departments such as art, physical education, social studies, English, science, mathematics, music, and special education. Meeting with the chairs of these departments helps principals keep current on district and state changes. Together, district leaders should explore curriculum summer projects to adjust to changing needs.

Personal Commentary/Notes: _____

_____

* Attend Meetings of Local Service Clubs

You've probably written a message to your local service clubs when school opened. Don't take them for granted. As principal, you have a responsibility to be the chief spokesperson for your school. Joining your area service clubs, sharing school news, and providing students to help with the clubs' activities often pay dividends in the form of donations of money and equipment and support for the local budget.

Principals also report that organizations such as Kiwanis, Rotary, Lions, and Elks provide speakers for career days, help to involve students in community service projects, and offer an opportunity to improve the school's public relations. These organizations send their own newsletters to the community and often include articles about your students and school. When your schedule makes it impossible for you to attend these meetings, ask another staff member to represent the middle school.

Personal Commentary/Notes: _____

_____

Review Bulletin Boards and School Exhibits *

Our elementary colleagues are experts in decorating their bulletin boards, halls, and classrooms. Middle school teachers should strive to make their building attractive and welcoming to guests and students. This becomes a little more difficult when teachers are forced to share classrooms. A feeling of ownership is lost in the process. However, we urge principals to develop ways to keep their bulletin boards current and attractive. Giving the art teacher a preparation period to achieve this objective may be worthwhile. The teacher can work with teams and departments to develop themes for each showcase and bulletin board. Some principals report that they encourage departments to change displays regularly, student clubs to advertise their activities, and parent organizations to help decorate the building.

Personal Commentary/Notes: _____

_____

Send Thank-You Notes After Open School Night *

Most principals have learned that they can never send enough thank-you notes. A good secretary can assist you to follow through in a consistent manner. Often, we take our best staff members for granted. A personal note mentioning how appreciative you are about their extraordinary effort helps to maintain their enthusiasm, and it may also serve as a keepsake for someone who appreciates your recognition.

Personal notes can also serve other needs, such as recognizing happy events with a congratulatory card or sending a sympathy note after a staff member's family tragedy. One principal from North Carolina told us that he has attended every faculty member's family funeral and every funeral for students' parents during the nine years he has headed the middle school.

Personal Commentary/Notes: _____

_____

* Update School Profile

Updating the school profile and the data fact sheet keeps the community members, the board of education, the superintendent, and your own staff current with information about the middle school. Often, our goals for the following year are based on the results of this school profile. And in contemporary times, local newspapers may also publish your testing results.

An excellent topic for a site-based team might be to analyze the data and make recommendations to address any areas of dissatisfaction. This can be a useful process even if your scores are excellent. It helps the faculty members to never take their past accomplishments for granted. Our goal should never focus on whom to blame but rather on how to solve problems. This message is an excellent tone setter for the review of one's school profile.

Personal Commentary/Notes: _____

_____

* Conduct Evening Social Activities for Students

Middle schools usually provide evening activities for their students. A listing of these events should go home regularly via the school newspaper, principal's newsletter, or the PTA meeting notices and minutes.

Supervision of these events is important. Parents want to know their children will be safe and enjoy an activity that is age appropriate. Parents may help as chaperones, but the staff must have the primary responsibility for keeping the event under control. Many teacher contracts mandate payment for this type of service. If not, the supervisory staff must seek volunteers to help. We recommend canceling any event where you question the adequacy of the supervision.

Personal Commentary/Notes: _____

_____

October Planning

* Prepare List of Capital Improvements

We mentioned the budget process in the key tasks; this now becomes a planning priority. Just as the district should maintain a five-year plan for the improvement of buildings and grounds, so too should the middle school principal. Items such as the roof should be listed with the following items noted:

- Date it was installed
- Present condition
- Cost of interim repairs
- Projected replacement date
- Estimated cost of replacement

This format should also be used for boilers, windows, hall flooring, and technology needs. Being specific with every request convinces the superintendent and board that you've done your homework. Poorly prepared wish lists get little consideration.

The following outline was submitted by a principal who wanted to modernize her library.

As part of the budgetary process and the introduction of new technology, the library is our prime consideration. Recent technological advances are revolutionizing this area and are adding new meaning to the title Library Media Center. Our library presently meets the needs of a generation of students who graduated decades ago. We have listed the items necessary to bring the middle school media center into the new century. Costs for each item are submitted at the end of the report.

- Computerized card catalogs and circulation systems
- CD-ROM-based reference tools, including electronic encyclopedias and magazine collections
- Electronic atlases, concordances, dictionaries, and almanacs
- Videodisc players with pictorial capabilities that can store entire collections of art
- A wide range of word-processing programs that allow students to create high-quality reports
- Online access to commercial databases and the World Wide Web via the Internet
- A wide range of educational materials designed to permit practice, tutorials, and simulations

---

This list will get larger each day. Think of this type of agenda for a site-based committee. Who would not be enthusiastic planning and researching for a future that is here?

Personal Commentary/Notes: _____

_____

* *Plan American Education Week Activities*

This is an excellent week to invite the community into your school and show them the best you have to offer. Showcase the programs and the talents of your students and staff. Post items about community service projects. Many principals prepare a handout that enlightens residents about the school and the purpose of middle school education. Don't lose the opportunity to highlight the band, science projects, and art portfolios. Your goal is to have parents go home feeling good about their school and American education. This week presents an opportune time to send a thank-you memo to the entire staff. (See Resource 18: American Education Week Memo.)

Personal Commentary/Notes: _____

_____

* *Join Principals' Associations*

Don't become so married to the job that you forget to broaden your perspectives. It is important to join local, state, and national organizations. Networking gives you a local support base and friendly colleagues to use as a sounding board about ideas and problems. Major organizations keep you informed about model programs and techniques being used in middle schools. Read journals, such as those published by the National Association of Secondary School Principals, to keep your knowledge current. Just as we encourage teachers to take inservice courses, we encourage principals to make learning a lifelong exercise.

Personal Commentary/Notes: _____

_____

October Personnel

* *Check on Teacher Observation Process*

Observing lessons now becomes a high priority for the middle school principal and the supervisory staff. Given the lifelong potential of tenure, observing new staff members is critical. If they are simply adequate, they should not be rehired. To build an excellent faculty, average is not good enough. We never give a nontenured teacher a third year, unless they are evaluated in their second year as being good to excellent. Perhaps the following vignette will help principals understand what seems to be a rigid set of standards:

Many years ago, a Long Island principal decided not to grant tenure to an adequate staff member. Her teammates came in and pleaded for her to be retained. The principal initially remained firm, but after many sessions with the team, he agreed to reverse himself. Tenure was granted. During the next decade, the teacher became his poorest staff member in that department and among the weakest teachers in the school. In the ten years that followed, the principal realized he exposed 1,250 students to an inferior teacher. He never made the mistake again. Excellence is its own reward. Excellence will never be achieved by the granting of tenure to adequate or average teachers and principals.

Personal Commentary/Notes: _____

_____

Host Breakfast for Staff *

This is your teacher appreciation morning. Parents will have a teacher recognition day later in the year, but a personal thank you is your responsibility. It is also a good way to bring the middle school faculty together since they usually revert to team relationships or departmental identification. Joining teachers at lunch is another way for principals to maintain a team atmosphere.

Personal Commentary/Notes: _____

_____

October Checklists

October Key Tasks

Major Assignments	Date Started	Date Completed	Days on Task
Set budget development timelines and parameters			
Review interim reports			
Prepare for Open School Night			
Plan Halloween dance and alternative activities			
Screen new entrants			
Review progress of students in need of special services			
Review plans for faculty meetings			
Hold first site-based committee meeting			
Coordinate the year's testing program			
Initiate grade-level plans			
Plan homecoming parade and activities			
Coordinate recognition day with board of education			
Conduct fire and emergency drills			

October Communications

✓	Assignment
	Plan monthly board of education presentation
	Help plan monthly PTA meetings
	Schedule K–12 principals' meetings
	Attend meetings of local service clubs
	Review bulletin boards and school exhibits
	Send thank-you notes after Open School Night
	Update school profile
	Conduct evening social activities for students

October Planning

✓	Assignment
	Prepare list of capital improvements
	Plan American Education Week activities
	Join principals' associations

October Personnel

✓	Finalize
	Check on teacher observation process
	Host breakfast for staff

October Calendar

MONTH: OCTOBER

YEAR: _____

MONDAY	TUESDAY	WEDNESDAY	THURSDAY	FRIDAY	SATURDAY / SUNDAY
MONDAY ____	TUESDAY ____	WEDNESDAY ____	THURSDAY ____	FRIDAY ____	SATURDAY ____ SUNDAY ____
MONDAY ____	TUESDAY ____	WEDNESDAY ____	THURSDAY ____	FRIDAY ____	SATURDAY ____ SUNDAY ____
MONDAY ____	TUESDAY ____	WEDNESDAY ____	THURSDAY ____	FRIDAY ____	SATURDAY ____ SUNDAY ____
MONDAY ____	TUESDAY ____	WEDNESDAY ____	THURSDAY ____	FRIDAY ____	SATURDAY ____ SUNDAY ____
MONDAY ____	TUESDAY ____	WEDNESDAY ____	THURSDAY ____	FRIDAY ____	SATURDAY ____ SUNDAY ____

NOTES _____

Chapter Five

Great things are not done by impulse, but by a series of small things brought together.

—Vincent van Gogh

n November, familiarity and routine should have replaced the hectic pace of the opening months of school. First-quarter report cards are a priority at this time. In most districts, ten weeks of school have been completed and parents are anxious to learn how their children are performing. The report card should be a comprehensive document, affording students and parents detailed information about conduct and achievement. Every few years, principals and site-based committees should collect report cards from other middle schools and compare them to their own. If others are superior, fine-tune yours. Remember, if you copy from one district, it's plagiarism. However, if you copy from many, it's educational scholarship!

We recognize that many states in the Sun Belt start school in August. In these cases, report cards might go out as early as October. Other adjustments might have to be made as we go through the school year. Fortunately, national holidays are consistent for schools, and November is associated with Thanksgiving.

Although promoting the academic environment is clearly a priority, this month culminates with the Thanksgiving Day holiday and vacation period. Thanksgiving affords middle schools a wonderful opportunity to develop schoolwide service projects. Many school districts across the United States are adopting community service requirements to qualify for high school diplomas. Many of us dedicated to middle school programs have long advocated community service as a means for adolescents to gain satisfaction from helping others and to practice good citizenship.

A principal from Indiana shared with us a poignant story about one of his students who was participating in their community service program. His responsibility was to read to a blind senior citizen who was quite infirm. His peers referred to her in a supportive way as his grandmother. During the third month of his service, the elderly woman died. The principal was brought to tears the following day when the student's classmates brought him sympathy cards and consoled him during lunch. That supportive tone can only be accomplished through community service.

November is also a time when classroom visitations are in full swing. Although we never minimize the importance of the evaluation process for all staff members, we urge that nontenured teachers be given priority. As stressed in October, to make staff and tenure recommendations, we must have done our homework thoroughly. Principals and chairpersons have only three or four months left to make these critical recommendations. Know your teachers' contract and observe faculty members early and often. Remember, you are the chief architect in building an exceptional staff.

November Key Tasks

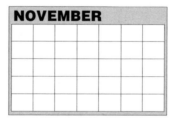

NOVEMBER

* *Prepare Report Cards*

The timeliness of report cards is an administrative function. Getting material to your staff, explaining how forms are to be filled in, and adhering to deadlines is the principal's—or his or her designee's—responsibility. Once these tasks are completed and report cards are ready for distribution, the principal should have a checklist of follow-up assignments to complete. Prior to the submission of grades, we recommend that the principal or another supervisor review them with each new teacher. This often avoids errors made by inexperienced teachers, and it may prevent a multitude of parental questions and complaints.

A simple check of the following items will help the principal maximize the purpose of grade reporting:

1. Have all teachers' grades reviewed by supervisors to note distribution data, number of failures, and conduct marks.

2. Ensure that counselors interview all students with multiple failures and students whose report cards indicate disciplinary problems.

3. Meet with each subject supervisor and review each teacher's grades.

4. Prepare parents for first report cards.

5. Analyze data, including number of failures, grade distribution, conduct marks, and attendance data.

6. Generate a list of students who qualify for the honor society and school-based recognition.

7. In the case of separated families, be sure to mail a copy of the report card to both parents if they each requested a copy and if both have a legal right to such reports.

Personal Commentary/Notes: _____

_____

Conduct Teacher Observations *

Make time in your schedule each week to conduct one or more formal observations and to informally visit a variety of classrooms. Management by walking around (MBWA) is an excellent means to assess the tone of individual classrooms and the academic environment of the entire school. Write a short note of thanks to teachers who are implementing positive learning experiences for their students.

In every text written about new teacher supervision, mentoring is viewed as extremely beneficial. This practice not only assists new teachers but also puts the talents of your old pros to use. And the veteran teachers benefit as well. Their morale is improved, and they feel their principal values their experience.

One area frequently forgotten is the need to notify the superintendent's office in the event of dissatisfaction with a teacher's performance. Sometimes the assistant superintendent is also called on to observe faculty members prior to their receiving a notification that they will not be rehired. With numerous court challenges instituted by discharged, nontenured teachers, this additional central office observation is highly recommended.

Personal Commentary/Notes: _____

_____

Hold Monthly Faculty Meeting *

Faculty meetings should not become routine and boring. If the meeting does not include a stimulating presentation or essential information, cancel it. Bring in experts or guest speakers to help make the meeting more productive and interesting.

A review of grading procedures in November is helpful. Having guidance counselors explain what they do when they meet with children who have failed subjects can help foster the team approach we seek to inculcate at the middle school level. Counselors should also visit team meetings and share appropriate information that they've received from student and parent contacts.

A middle school principal from Nevada dedicated all faculty meetings during one year to having each department explain their curriculum to other staff members by giving mini-lessons and distributing a summary of their course topics. This enhanced departmental pride and helped interdepartmental teams to develop more sophisticated team projects. The faculty meeting is the principal's lesson plan and should serve as a model of professional expertise.

Personal Commentary/Notes: _____

_____

✷ *Preview School Play*

If your drama club or art department presents an annual school play, the principal should determine if the material is age appropriate. This should be done before the choice of a play is announced. A play is a wonderful opportunity to showcase the talents of your students and staff. Many districts invite senior citizens' groups to attend the performance free of charge. This becomes a valuable part of your public relations (PR) effort.

This is also the time to discuss the holiday music selections. Many schools create wonderful performances only to be criticized for music that was too religious or not religious enough. If the district has a music director, principals should try to use his or her expertise in this matter. If the issue becomes emotionally overloaded, the parents' association could serve as an advisory group.

Personal Commentary/Notes: _____

_____

✷ *Encourage Schoolwide Service Projects*

Remember that service to the community is a goal of middle-level education. We should assist the district's residents to learn that middle schools educate the whole child. November is a perfect time to have food collections for the needy. Our students are not shy about going to local merchants and getting donations of free turkeys and canned goods.

Principals report success in working cooperatively with community service groups. These volunteers provide additional funds for the purchase of food and also award children with letters of appreciation and plaques for their participation. There is one caution regarding food collection, however: Names of the recipients should be confidential since often the gifts go to families of your own student body. With this concern in mind, students should be involved in the collection but not in the distribution of the holiday dinners. Sending a letter to local merchants concerning the upcoming drive is an excellent way to legitimize the event for all concerned.

Personal Commentary/Notes: _____

_____

Review Fundraising Guidelines *

The National Association of Secondary School Principals (NASSP), Department of Student Activities, provides the following fundraising guidelines:

Before you begin a fundraising program:

1. Meet with the person-in-charge to:
   a. Discuss procedures.
   b. Reserve a date on the fundraising calendar.
   c. Review the financial requirements.
   d. Complete all required forms.
   e. Submit all pertinent information regarding the company with which you plan to deal.
   f. Secure approval for your project.

2. Secure a list of fundraising participants.

3. Turn in money collected to the person-in-charge on a daily or preset schedule.

4. Sign and turn in a "Request for Check" form with invoices and/or receipts. (See Resource 19: Fundraising Considerations.)

SOURCE: From Laird, J. (1995). *Survival guide.* Reston, VA: National Association of Secondary School Principals.

Personal Commentary/Notes: _____

November Communications

Prepare PTA Presentation *

Use your presentation time to share plans concerning upcoming events. Call for volunteers if help is needed either in the planning or the hosting of the activity. Parents feel a part of the school when they are involved in important projects and events.

This is also an opportunity to explain the report card information to parents. Explain the line of communication they should use if a problem occurs. State clearly to parents that if they are concerned about a grade or teacher, they should see the teacher first. If they are not satisfied with the conference, then they should feel free to meet with the subject supervisor. If that meeting is unsatisfactory, they should make an appointment with the principal. We have found that nearly 95% of concerns are settled amicably at the teacher conference level.

Many principals prefer to involve the counselor immediately. They feel that parent concerns can be communicated to the teacher in a calmer manner by a colleague. Either way, the principal should discuss his or her system of communication with the PTA and the faculty. New teachers might need the assistance of mentors or supervisors if they have difficult parent conferences. This topic is important enough to include in the new teacher orientation program.

Personal Commentary/Notes: _____

_____

* Compose Holiday School Policy Memo

Beside musical selections, holidays have other potential problems. Recently, issues have been raised about decorations, sales, and in-school parties. Principals must know their board of education's policies regarding these matters. A reminder memo to all staff each year outlining the key expectations helps to avoid future problems.

Most principals allow parties in their school classrooms, but they are held after school. They also require a cleanup committee to work after the party. With this procedure, education remains the school's primary mission.

Personal Commentary/Notes: _____

_____

* Prepare Board of Education Presentation

Many principals have a good news box located somewhere in the main office or teachers' room. In preparing a board presentation, these items and other bits of good news can be incorporated into the speech. The board relishes the opportunity to recognize student achievements and faculty accomplishments. The meeting provides an exceptional PR platform. Take advantage of the chance to advertise activities for November and December.

Personal Commentary/Notes: _____

_____

Foster Appreciation of Religious and Cultural Diversity *

This is not only a topic for the holiday season but a national priority. Since the new century began, the fifty largest American cities have minorities as their majority population. Your school probably serves one or more minority groups. In some New York City schools, the number of diverse ethnic groups is even higher. Use the holiday and the instructional program to promote cultural diversity and an appreciation of a variety of religions. Minority members' contributions to our society are not just a topic for social studies but should be part of your school's program, along with intercultural activities. Events such as Unity Days and Ethnic Foods Night and hall displays should be used to make everyone feel welcomed in your middle school.

Personal Commentary/Notes: _____

_____

Initiate Student Service Awards Program *

Middle schools were first to develop the Student of the Month Award. The local press is usually provided with a picture of the child and a brief description about why he or she was selected. These programs promote school spirit and put the school in a positive light. Announcing the child's name over the public address system adds to the publicity and student pride. Many middle schools select a student of the month from each team. This makes it possible for weaker students, who have shown improvement, to win the honor, which is key to the motivation of all students.

Personal Commentary/Notes: _____

_____

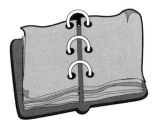

November Planning

Review Procedures *
for Inclement Weather

Although we planned for bad weather and emergencies when we opened school, these procedures should be reviewed as we enter the winter months. Many districts use delayed openings in inclement weather. The principal should publish new time schedules for both one- and two-hour delayed openings. Most administrators simply modify the regular schedule, reducing each period by five minutes for a one-hour delay and ten minutes for a two-hour delay. Homeroom is extended to give both teachers and students an opportunity to arrive for classes.

In advance of bad weather, school districts should let parents know which radio and television stations will carry school closings and delayed openings. November is the time to use the emergency telephone chains we distributed to staff and parents in September. Principals frequently make personal calls to teachers who live very far from school to prevent the possibility that the teacher will leave for school prior to receiving the school closing announcement via the normal emergency phone chain.

Personal Commentary/Notes: _____

_____

* Apply for Funds and Permission to Attend Conferences

Principals who don't plan to attend an occasional conference may become overly immersed in the operations of their building. It's critical to your personal and professional renewal to attend educational conferences to recharge your battery. Reading journals is recommended, but nothing replaces face-to-face meetings with colleagues and attendance at workshops. National conferences are held throughout the year, and it is a good idea to attend one or two each year. You may also want to be a presenter and share some of your school's model programs.

For those principals who cannot bear to be away when school is in session, excellent conferences are held in the summer. NASSP programs and college institutes are offered in July and August. All of us need to have our horizons expanded.

Personal Commentary/Notes: _____

_____

* Complete Enrollment Projections

The complexity of this task depends on your community. In stable neighborhoods, a principal is able to simply carry over the number of children in each grade. A few calls to the elementary principals will produce an accurate number for your incoming sixth grade. However, other principals may have to deal with a more transient community—people moving in and out during the summer and throughout the school year. Large numbers of children may go to private and parochial schools after sixth or seventh grade. Call on the assistant superintendent of personnel for assistance in gathering enrollment figures. Since the number may affect staffing for the following year, it is not a task to delegate. Our goal is to flag changes for the central office rather than having to make last-minute staffing changes.

Personal Commentary/Notes: _____

_____

Schedule Holiday and Community Service Events *

Very soon the school will be on center stage for the holiday celebrations. The principal's plans should include all of the following:

- Involve the PTA in such activities as the holiday book fair, flea markets, special lunches, and teacher recognition days.
- Send invitations to senior citizens' groups.
- Work cooperatively with community service organizations concerning holiday food drives, which can be held in both November and December and may require dual plans.
- Contact the Marine Corps to indicate your desire to participate in their Toys-for-Tots campaign. (See Resource 20: Principal's Newsletter to Parents.)

Personal Commentary/Notes: _____

_____

November Personnel

Involve the Library/Media Center *

The library should be the hub of a middle school program. Involve the librarian on team projects. The librarian should act as a resource for curriculum areas. Promote the use of the media center and use the professional qualifications of the librarian to help the quality of our interdepartmental projects. Conducting a book fair in December ensures some educational gifts are exchanged during the holidays.

Personal Commentary/Notes: _____

_____

Continue New Teacher Orientation *

The group aspects of our orientation program are coming to a close, and the intensity of the program is subsiding. More time will be spent with teachers who are struggling than with those who are adjusting to the demands of the job. During November, principals should review report card procedures and discuss grading of students' projects. New teachers should also be prepared for the approaching holidays and be advised to maintain discipline.

Personal Commentary/Notes: _____

_____

November Checklists

November Key Tasks

Major Assignments	Date Started	Date Completed	Days on Task
Prepare report cards			
Conduct teacher observations			
Hold monthly faculty meeting			
Preview school play			
Encourage schoolwide service projects			
Review fundraising guidelines			

November Communications

✓	Assignment
	Prepare PTA presentation
	Compose holiday school policy memo
	Prepare board of education presentation
	Foster appreciation of religious and culture diversity
	Initiate student service awards program

November Planning

✓	Assignment
	Review procedures for inclement weather
	Apply for funds and permission to attend conferences
	Complete enrollment projections
	Schedule holiday and community service events

November Personnel

✓	Finalize
	Involve the library/media center
	Continue new teacher orientation

November Calendar

MONTH: NOVEMBER

YEAR: _____

MONDAY	TUESDAY	WEDNESDAY	THURSDAY	FRIDAY	SATURDAY
					SUNDAY
					SATURDAY
					SUNDAY
					SATURDAY
					SUNDAY
					SATURDAY
					SUNDAY
					SATURDAY
					SUNDAY

NOTES _____

Chapter Six

December

If you wish your merit to be known, acknowledge that of other people.

—Asian proverb

December is a high-visibility month for your school and staff. There are numerous functions that involve students. The winter concert is usually well attended and fully appreciated by the school community. Many principals invite grandparents and senior citizens to the last dress rehearsal held during the school day, which helps decrease the crowd at the evening concert, provides excellent public relations (PR) for the middle school, and serves as a final dress rehearsal.

If you permit school parties, we have several strong recommendations. First, they should not be held during the school day. Nothing should adversely affect the academic tone in the school, and a party atmosphere certainly detracts from a businesslike environment. Second, if parties are held after school, the principal should be notified and furnished with the names of the students on the cleanup committee. The custodian should not have to reclean the classrooms. Finally, we recommend that these events be restricted to one hour so that students do not miss late buses or have to walk home in the dark. Education, health, and safety are always priorities.

Three other popular activities that often occur in December include the book fair, the holiday gift shop, and the collection of toys and clothing for the needy. If the PTA hosts the book fair and the gift shop, then the staff members are given the opportunity to make a statement about the kinds of gifts they would encourage parents to purchase for the holidays. Presents such as books, stamp albums, science kits, and rock collections are more meaningful than pop culture items.

Don't neglect the opportunity to engage in community service during the holiday period. Students should visit nursing homes or collect food for less-fortunate families. This is an additional way to enhance the true spirit of the holidays. Educators should encourage children to experience the joy of giving since too often during the holidays they focus on receiving gifts.

When we express our concern about the tone of the school, just prior to the winter recess, we must warn our faculty about relaxing their demands. They too are going on vacation, but the principal must urge everyone to focus on education. This is not easy when children are engaged in fun holiday activities outside of school and are excused for chorus, orchestra, and band rehearsals. December is a good time for the principal to be visible in the halls, cafeteria, and classrooms—using the management by walking around (MBWA) technique—to keep the staff and students focused on academics.

As we note in our key tasks, the vacation period for teachers is not necessarily a holiday for your custodians. Establish work objectives with your head custodian; especially include tasks that cannot be done when children are in the school. The painting of corridors and classrooms and the construction of bookcases in classrooms are examples of jobs that need to be done when the students are on vacation. The washing and polishing of floors is a minimal expectation.

A few safety concerns should be raised at this time regarding legal requirements and safety plans for the postholiday period. Check fire inspection requirements because many states mandate that letters of compliance be sent at the end of December and again in June. In addition to possible vandalism, security of the building when it is not in use must be discussed with the staff.

Setting schedules for midterm examinations should not await your return in January. Copies of all formal or departmental exams should be submitted in December and reviewed by the appropriate chairperson or building supervisor. If secretaries work over the holiday, they may have the opportunity to duplicate the tests for use in January. Here, too, providing security to safeguard the examinations is a responsibility of the administrative staff. A large safe, if available, or locked file cabinets should be used to secure the test papers.

One principal designed a work schedule for his secretaries who work during the holiday vacation. They are assigned the following tasks:

- Duplicate the principal's welcome-back letter for January.
- Write thank-you notes to students, staff, and parents for their help during the first four months of the school year.
- Prepare and place in teacher mailboxes a welcome-back memorandum that highlights coming events for January.
- Organize the midyear report card data collection forms.
- Take down holiday decorations and make the office ready for the new year.

Although the principal needs a well-deserved vacation, make sure everything is in place for the first school day in January.

December Key Tasks

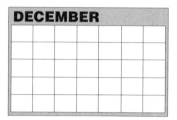

DECEMBER

* *Plan Holiday Work Schedule With Head Custodian*

Knowledge of the specifics of our custodians' jobs is a topic that is not emphasized in most administrative programs. In our resource section, we have included the many components of the head custodian's job responsibilities, which can be addressed during the holidays. (See Resource 23: Rating Scale for Custodial Services.) These itemized tasks could serve as an inservice course for many school leaders. Simply discussing each task with your head custodian will convince him or her about your attention to detail and provide a meaningful work schedule for the vacation period.

Just as we set a tone of expectations for our teachers and students, we should provide motivation for our cleaners and maintainers. In this way, principals are sure that the building will be ready for the second semester. Completed projects will be noted by your returning staff members and should reinforce that others contribute to the learning environment.

Personal Commentary/Notes: _____

_____

* *Review Budget Proposals*

The cost of educating children in the United States increases every year. Principals must work with their board of education and superintendent by providing a clear and specific justification for every budgetary request. Stating the need for a requested item usually increases the likelihood that the request will be fulfilled. If the material will be used to enhance the curriculum or assist in raising test scores, full consideration will be given to your wish list. The budget is a key task until March or April in most districts. If the district's budget is voted on in May, you can be certain that the board and superintendent will require all information a full month earlier. In most cases, health and safety items gain approval while additional staffing has to be fully justified. Personnel costs have become more than 70% of most budgets. For most principals, it seems that as salaries and health benefits have increased, it has become more difficult to have other necessities approved.

This is why we recommend that principals have systems to help them do the following tasks:

- Monitor materials and supplies.
- Strictly enforce rules for the return of textbooks.
- Support the librarian's efforts to collect books and fines.
- Double-check on the use and abuse of duplicating machines.
- Be sure that groups using the school are not vandalizing the building.

Personal Commentary/Notes: _____

_____

Complete and Report Calendar Year Fire Drills *

As stated at the beginning of this chapter, check to see that you complete all drills and report the data to the proper agency. Many school districts are located in cold climates. If this is the case, fire drills should be held early in the school year. Every principal must know the number of drills to be completed by the end of December.

Personal Commentary/Notes: _____

_____

Conduct Faculty Meeting *

The December faculty meeting is an appropriate time to celebrate with your staff and give thanks for their efforts during the first four months of the school year. It's also an excellent time to express your expectations for continuing the academic tone of the school. Let staff know that there will be many interruptions due to special events, but their classrooms should be as businesslike as possible. This requires a leader whose philosophy is to maintain education as the school's top priority.

Personal Commentary/Notes: _____

_____

Schedule Classroom Observations *

All nontenured staff should have been observed twice by the end of December. Those experiencing difficulty may have been reviewed more often. By the start of next month, the assistant superintendent for personnel may be asking the principal for tentative staffing recommendations. Any teacher whose rehiring is in question should be scheduled for additional observations. Knowing this, the principal can direct other supervisors to visit the teacher as well. Ultimately, the principal has to make the decision to award tenure but should do so with maximum input from his administrative team. Harsh as it may sound, when in doubt, do not rehire.

Personal Commentary/Notes: _____

_____

* *Preview Holiday or Variety Show*

Many schools hold some type of student variety show. We much prefer the holiday concert, which features a larger number of students and highlights the chorus, orchestra, and band. This month includes so many activities that we recommend putting off other events until the spring semester or when a boost in student morale is necessary. If the principal chooses to host a variety show, make sure that proper supervision is provided and that acts are previewed to avoid inappropriate material or behavior.

Personal Commentary/Notes: _____

_____

* *Determine Components of the Sixth-Grade Orientation Program*

It is not too early to begin planning the following year's sixth-grade orientation. Principals can visit the present sixth graders and ask them what they found most helpful in the orientation program they experienced. With this in mind, specific elements can be developed for implementation in May or June. Some specifics include the following:

1. Invite parents of fifth graders to a night meeting.

2. Invite fifth graders to visit the middle school building:
   - Host an assembly.
   - Use student guides to show classrooms.
   - Hold a question-and-answer period at the end of the day.

3. Have counselors visit every fifth-grade class:
   - Explain how to read a middle school schedule.
   - Demonstrate how to open a combination lock.
   - Explain the function of the guidance department.
   - Discuss extracurricular activities open to middle school students.

4. Meet with elementary teachers:
   - Discuss atypical children.
   - Note those with special needs or accommodations.
   - Get recommendations of students who should or should not be placed in the same classes.

5. Bring new sixth graders in a day early to show them their schedules and classrooms.

Personal Commentary/Notes: _____

_____

December Communications

Prepare PTA Presentation *

Many middle school PTAs host a faculty recognition day luncheon prior to the winter recess. We have found that teachers and staff appreciate the PTA's congeniality and the buffet lunch. The tone is cordial and brings out the *P* in PTA.

Active parent organizations sponsor book fairs and other fundraising events. Principals support their efforts since books make excellent holiday gifts. Bob Ricken sends home an annual holiday message to parents, titled "Holiday Gifts: A Challenge or a Burden." We have included the letter in our resource section. (See Resource 21: Holiday Gifts: A Challenge or a Burden.)

Personal Commentary/Notes: _____

_____

Prepare Presentation for Board of Education Meeting *

Principals are always wise to anticipate problems and inform the superintendent about them prior to the monthly board meeting. In this way, principals minimize surprises and the superintendent has time to prepare a response to questions in an appropriate and thoughtful manner. Consequently, the principal is truly part of the superintendent's team.

Many complaints or concerns are raised at PTA meetings. If principals are not able to resolve them at the building level, there is a good chance they will be raised at a board meeting. A respectful relationship with PTA leaders helps to keep issues in-house. This is where the principal's credibility and expertise help to keep minor problems from becoming major ones.

All middle school performing groups are preparing for their winter concerts, and the December board meeting is a good time to showcase one of the groups. This guarantees a large turnout for the meeting at a time when people are involved with holiday preparations.

Personal Commentary/Notes: _____

_____

✳ *Prepare for Retirement Parties*

A principal from Minnesota sent in this additional December key task. She felt that teachers should have a grand send-off after thirty years in the profession. She organizes these events with key faculty and writes letters to public officials, including the president of the United States, to request an acknowledgment for the service rendered by each retiree. The other details are performed by a faculty committee that decides the place for the party, the costs, and the program. When letters of congratulations are read from the president, the governor, and other local officials, it makes the event more memorable.

Personal Commentary/Notes: _____

_____

December Planning

✳ *Prepare Standardized Test Results*

Prepare to mail home a copy of any standardized test results to each parent. This may be added to your secretary's holiday vacation work schedule. An accompanying letter should assist parents with the interpretation of the scores. The correspondence can also instruct parents to refer any questions to the appropriate teacher or counselor. One thing is certain in this current era of assessment: There will be more rather than less testing.

Personal Commentary/Notes: _____

_____

✳ *Devise Midyear Examination Schedule*

With the proliferation of mandated examinations, some middle schools have eliminated formal midterms. We strongly recommend finals in all semester and ten-week courses. They may be held in class or be part of the midterm schedule. The elimination of midterms strikes at the heart of middle school philosophy—much of traditional middle school activities is being limited by today's accountability emphasis. Formal standardized tests are not the only way to evaluate children and programs, and middle school principals should be debating the testing issue at conferences and at the state policy-making level.

Personal Commentary/Notes: _____

_____

Review Winter Concert Schedule *

Monitor the December calendar carefully. It quickly fills up and easily conflicts with other school and community-wide events. Review the program for length and content. Know your board of education's policy concerning holidays, decorations, and religious symbols. Some districts have used this period as a statement for their support of separation of church and state.

Invitations to parents should be sent home and reminders about such items as cell phones, cameras, and recording devices should be included. Unfortunately, parents and students need a review of auditorium behavior and etiquette. If the middle school auditorium is too small, arrangements should be made for the use of the district's high school, which will require a dress rehearsal and possibly busing if you also have a school day concert at the middle school.

Personal Commentary/Notes: _____

_____

Conduct Midyear Locker Cleanup *

We recommend locker cleanups prior to every extended holiday and at the close of the school year. Custodians should be stationed with large trash cans in each corridor, so students can easily discard unwanted items. It's helpful to have the homeroom or classroom teachers supervise the entire process. We find that many lost coats, sweaters, and texts are found. So too are many uneaten lunches.

Personal Commentary/Notes: _____

_____

December Personnel

Coordinate Purchase of Gifts * for Office and Custodial Staff

Many teachers receive gifts from parents and students. If there is a board policy concerning gift giving and receiving, adhere to its provisions. Many staff members give token gifts to custodians, aides, and secretaries. These expressions of recognition are appreciated by those whose hard work makes our jobs easier. Some districts allow only donations to charity in a person's name and prohibit the entire gift-giving process. Most principals whom we've interviewed give presents to their secretaries unless gift giving is forbidden by board policy.

Personal Commentary/Notes: _____

_____

★ Review Extracurricular Activities and Evaluate Advisors and Coaches

Every staff member who directs an extracurricular activity should receive an evaluation, a frequently overlooked supervisory responsibility. Teachers working under a contract usually need evidence of poor performance before being relieved of duty as advisors or coaches. One additional personnel matter is the hiring for the second half of the year. Review coaches with the director of athletics and discuss club assignments with supervisors and assistant principals. Be consistent with the terms of all contracts and with board policy when hiring or recommending the staff replacements.

Personal Commentary/Notes: _____

_____

December Checklists

December Key Tasks

Major Assignments	Date Started	Date Completed	Days on Task
Plan holiday work schedule with head custodian			
Review budget proposals			
Complete and report calendar year fire drills			
Conduct faculty meeting			
Schedule classroom observations			
Preview holiday or variety show			
Determine components of the sixth-grade orientation program			

December Communications

✔	Assignment
	Prepare PTA presentation
	Prepare presentation for board of education meeting
	Prepare for retirement parties

December Planning

✓	Assignment
	Prepare standardized test results
	Devise midyear examination schedule
	Review winter concert schedule
	Conduct midyear locker cleanup

December Personnel

✓	Finalize
	Coordinate purchase of gifts for office and custodial staff
	Review extracurricular activities and evaluate advisors and coaches

December Calendar

MONTH: DECEMBER

YEAR: ____

MONDAY	TUESDAY	WEDNESDAY	THURSDAY	FRIDAY	SATURDAY
					SUNDAY
					SATURDAY
					SUNDAY
					SATURDAY
					SUNDAY
					SATURDAY
					SUNDAY
					SATURDAY
					SUNDAY

NOTES

____

103

Chapter Seven

To be good is noble, but to teach others how to be good is nobler.

—Mark Twain

Now that the winter recess is over, the building principal should reestablish a businesslike set of expectations for the staff and the student body. A tone-setting welcome-back presentation via the public address system and visits to classrooms are techniques often employed by school leaders for this purpose. Remind students that this is the end of the first semester and urge them to prepare for midterm examinations with a clear and demanding, yet caring, message. Emphasize that in subjects such as art, technology, and home and careers, these examinations will serve as their finals.

The principal should be organizing both the end-of-first-semester activities and the second-semester schedules and staffing. Performing these tasks is an excellent example of how the administrator must operate in the present while always being cognizant of the forthcoming month, semester plans, and activities. If the school is to remain calm and orderly, the principal's organizational skills must be in full use, and the principal must stay focused. As we stressed earlier, completing the month's key tasks is critical to a principal's success. Intent is admirable, but principals will not achieve a functional environment without detailed planning.

All first-semester staff evaluations should be completed in a timely fashion. By now, the supervisory staff should be able to list teachers whose professional performance is in need of improvement. In the following two or three months, constructive plans can be offered to assist these teachers. Principals should know about any inadequacies in teachers' performance in January and participate in the development of new supervisory plans. The central office must be made aware of the steps taken to help struggling staff members. If attempts to help fail, then the principal has a paper trail documenting the remediation efforts. In this manner, there will be no surprises, and teachers will be informed prior to spring recess if they are to be terminated.

Many schools hold parent conferences at this time, though some prefer the event take place in February after the receipt of midyear report cards. This is an individual principal's decision, usually made with staff input. Parents have a right to be informed about their child's progress, particularly if the student is experiencing academic or behavioral difficulties. We must do more than pay lip service to teacher-parent collaboration. Parental notification of a child's problem eliminates the possibility that the parent will feel they were not adequately informed. Communication between home and school is essential if we want to concentrate on helping the child. Failure to do this in a timely fashion is an invitation to accusations, blame, and confrontation. Letters, interim reports, conferences, and telephone calls must be employed to accomplish effective communication.

JANUARY

January Key Tasks

Review Teacher *
Performance Evaluations

The process of staff evaluations should be in full swing. Evidence of instruction, in the form of written reviews of lesson plans, should be given to the principal and also filed with appropriate central office administrators. Midyear is the time to review each faculty member's evaluation.

The principal should meet with every supervisor to ensure there are specific instructional plans for each teacher. This is also a way to evaluate the quality of every supervisor's written evaluations. Make certain that all administrators reviewing a teacher's lesson are focused on the same remediation techniques.

Nontenured teachers need intensive training and evaluations. Principals should meet privately with each of them to build on the teacher's strengths and to address all concerns. For those who are not performing well, the specific areas that must be improved should be stated verbally and in writing. For those who are progressing in a highly efficient manner, the principal should also feel free to give positive affirmation of their performance in writing. These are the teachers who will become the quality members of your staff in the future. (See Resource 22: Administrator's Observation Worksheet.)

Personal Commentary/Notes: _____

_____

* Create Remedial Plans for Staff

Don't take your tenured teachers for granted. All teachers need positive feedback and constructive suggestions about areas and techniques in need of improvement. Having superior staff members model lessons for other teachers helps make the improvement of instruction a goal for everyone. No matter how good a teacher's evaluation, every faculty member should have a staff development plan in place. Awareness of your teachers' needs is important in determining who should attend specific conferences and workshops.

One additional word is necessary about your outstanding teachers: Involving them as mentors is a minimal expectation. Individual conferences should be held with each of these teachers to explore creative ways they might help other staff members. The principal may wish to encourage them to go into guidance or administration. In Mineola Middle School in New York, during a fifteen-year period, twenty staff members became principals, assistant principals, subject area directors, counselors, psychologists, and social workers. This is obvious evidence of a staff development program.

Personal Commentary/Notes: _____

_____

* Evaluate Custodial Staff

When we speak of *staff*, we include everyone who works in the building, whereas when we say the word *faculty*, we refer solely to teachers. At this time, it's appropriate to give a midyear evaluation to the custodial staff. Many of us feel somewhat inadequate evaluating our nonprofessional employees. However, it is as important for them to receive an assessment of their performance as it is for the faculty members. We have included a form to be used to evaluate these important employees. (See Resource 23: Rating Scale for Custodial Services.)

Personal Commentary/Notes: _____

_____

* Distribute Midyear Report Cards

The end of this month coincides with the conclusion of the second marking period. It also is, as noted previously, the final grading period for ten- and twenty-week courses. All teachers should be given timelines for the distribution of report cards in February. This will enable them to plan their testing schedules, calculate grades, and hand in their marks in a timely fashion. The required dates should be noted on the principal's weekly memo to staff.

Teachers should be encouraged to contact the parents of students who may possibly fail or whose behavior in class has deteriorated. Once again, the counselors' role is critical in the communication process. The guidance staff should interview all students with multiple failures and call the parents of students who may have to go to summer school or repeat the grade. These suggestions are further detailed in February.

Personal Commentary/Notes: _____

_____

Review Department and Team Goals *

Meet with every chairperson or department supervisor to review progress toward achievement of department goals. Goals should be specific and driven by student achievement data. Limit the number of goals and make them substantive—more is not necessarily better. Goals, if properly designed, should fit into an overall school context and philosophy that the principal is responsible for establishing and monitoring. In this age of accountability, goals probably will be based on the performance of students during the last state or district examination.

A meeting with each school team should accomplish the same task. In this way, the principal can determine the progress toward goals and assist the team if they want to readjust their goals. It's also another opportunity to meet in small groups with faculty members. Sharing concerns of others keeps the principal abreast of potential problems. Team members might also share information about individual children. These face-to-face meetings reduce the number of surprises and keep everyone student oriented and focused.

Personal Commentary/Notes: _____

_____

Review Curriculum Initiatives *

As part of the budget process, new course proposals and revisions should be submitted to the superintendent for approval. These new and revised courses will affect the budget and future curriculum improvement. Teachers, team leaders, and departmental supervisors should be reminded that requests for modification of curriculum must be recommended early if the changes are to be implemented during the following year.

The principal should meet with subject area leaders and the assistant superintendent for curriculum to remain informed about changes in curriculum mandates. Most states have online curriculum regulations that can be accessed on a personal computer. This is another reason why principals should attend conferences. It's inexcusable for the district's curriculum not to reflect the latest in state requirements.

Personal Commentary/Notes: _____

_____

* Finalize Budget Requests

Most items in a middle school budget will be submitted at the end of January or in early February. This allows time for the review of every proposal and the consideration of cost factors. A careful examination of the budget calendar indicates not only due dates but also meetings where the principal is allowed the opportunity to defend each submission. Preparation for these meetings must be vigorous and comprehensive if the principal hopes to have the item included in the following year's budget. Supporting arguments about the relevancy of the requested items to state mandates, health and safety issues, and the district's goals are most persuasive. Carefully prepared computer-generated presentations are usually well received by the board and the superintendent.

Personal Commentary/Notes: _____

_____

* Make Informal Class Visits

The principal who is visible is seen as being available. Children recognize the school leader and report to parents that they saw him or her in the halls or in the classroom. More important, faculty members do not lose contact with the principal. The larger the building, the more important these brief classroom visits become. Teachers get caught up in their own schedules, team meetings, building assignments, and departmental meetings. Informal visits and conversations often pay a multitude of dividends. Sometimes teachers ask to see the principal later about a personal concern, which can keep a small issue from snowballing. In no way does this meeting replace the regular supervisory visit or classroom observation.

Personal Commentary/Notes: _____

_____

* Conduct Faculty Meeting

We generally frown on holding faculty meetings to discuss issues that could be handled through paper correspondence. However, there are several January tasks that must be completed in a timely manner for the school to close the books on the first half of the year. The principal should personally oversee the following:

- Responsibility for the development of midterms for yearlong courses and finals for ten- and twenty-week courses
- Security provision for examination papers
- Storage of examination papers after they are graded
- Grading procedures and due dates for report cards

Since most states require a variety of inservice staff training, evidence of compliance for these topics must be provided. Such issues as right-to-know laws, sexual harassment, child abuse, and special education accommodations are examples of topics that must be presented to the entire faculty. Some mandates require annual review. Once the staff receives the training, a notice should be sent to the superintendent, whose office is responsible for informing state officials.

Personal Commentary/Notes: _____

_____

Prepare for Winter Examinations *

Many middle schools have ceased to have a formal examination schedule in January, opting instead for in-class examinations. This allows instruction to continue in classes where there are no examinations. If there is a formal schedule, proctors should be given some inservice training, and expectations for student behavior should be discussed in classes. We prefer not to opt for a high school–type of plan, which often includes release time for students who are not being tested.

Personal Commentary/Notes: _____

_____

January Communications

*Conduct Parent-Teacher * Conferences*

Many principals prefer to hold their parent-teacher conferences after the second report card is issued in February. We encourage as many contacts as possible between the school and the home. Teacher contracts may limit the number of formal parent conferences to one or two a year. This is unfortunate, but contractual provisions must be honored. If conferences are limited, principals should require staff members to contact all parents whose children are in danger of failing. This can be done with written forms or personal phone calls.

If there are regularly scheduled conferences, the principal should prepare parents for the purpose and function of the conference. In case of large parental turnout, a follow-up conference can be scheduled for a later date. Again, if the conference does not go well, parents should be instructed to see the subject supervisor. Parents who are not satisfied with their meetings with the teacher or supervisor should be encouraged to see the principal. The door to the principal's office should remain open in the event of an unresolved issue.

Personal Commentary/Notes: _____

_____

* Coordinate PTA Presentation

This is an opportune time to prepare parents for the January-February changeover from one semester to another. During the presentation, you can address specific issues related to the change, such as the following: Students may be scheduled for one or more different classes; parents' questions about their child's grades; and which grades count on the high school record. A word or two about the parent-teacher conference is appropriate as well.

Personal Commentary/Notes: _____

_____

* Prepare for Board of Education Meeting

Principals have a variety of topics they can present at the January board of education meeting. An end-of-semester report that highlights staff and student accomplishments will maintain the flow of information between the middle school and the community. It's a good time to feature the art, home and careers, and technology programs since many students will be taking one of those classes for the first time in February. Some examples of student work from those subjects often make for an interesting display.

Personal Commentary/Notes: _____

_____

* Obtain Feedback on Student Lunch Program

Some principals distribute brief questionnaires about the school lunch program. Students are asked which meals they like best and which meals are unpopular. School dietitians are limited in what they can offer, and they are frequently forced to keep prices down. Any improvement the principal can make is greatly appreciated by children and staff. The following poem captures complaints about one school lunch program.

School lunch is great in September

Good in October

Fair in November

Bearable in December

Dull in January

Poor in February

Bad in March

Awful in April

Disgusting in May

Inedible in June

SOURCE: Ricken, R. (1984). *Love me when I'm most unlovable: The middle school years.* Reston, VA: National Association of Secondary School Principals.

Nevertheless, we recommend contact with students and the school's cook during the school year. This is the best time to rate the meals of the first semester and think of ways to improve the menu from February to June. Most middle school students do not go out for lunch and thus are a captured audience. Since most schools are instructed to limit candy and cake for nutritional reasons, lunches are even less attractive in the eyes of many youngsters.

Personal Commentary/Notes: _____

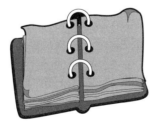

January Planning

Assess Sixth-Grade ✱ Orientation Program

By midyear, the orientation program should be just about completed. Ask the students who just went through the process to evaluate what was helpful, what was unnecessary, and what could be improved. Counselors may have suggestions since they were closely involved in conducting workshops in the elementary school, meeting with parents of fifth graders, and, most important, handling the concerns of our youngest students when school began in September.

Most principals keep the feedback in a folder titled "Sixth-Grade Orientation Program." Suggestions to improve the existing program can be heeded, and humorous comments can be used when we next meet with parents of future sixth graders or at the class's moving-up exercise, which occurs in eighth grade—a mere two and a half years away.

Personal Commentary/Notes: _____

_____

* *Review Ongoing Grants*

We hope this reminder touches a guilty nerve. Many grants are available to supplement existing programs and develop new initiatives. Some principals have the services of an administrative intern, and grant applications can be a challenging assignment for an intern and his or her supervising principal. However, remember to monitor all grant deadlines that you presently have and be sure that all available resources are used. Due dates for grant renewals should be in your monthly calendar preceding the deadline.

We found that networking with other principals helps principals learn about other opportunities. Some districts employ a grant writer, who can provide you with ideas, deadlines, and state or private funding priorities. Perusing journals for requests for proposals (RFPs) can help you find available grants. Sometimes the district's own teachers' union offers mini-grants to its staff members.

Personal Commentary/Notes: _____

_____

* *Monitor Bulletin Board Displays*

The first items visitors observe when visiting a middle school are the hall and bulletin board displays. As we approach the second half of the year, reminders should be sent to departments and teams about updating their displays. Some principals assign an art teacher to assist departments with their bulletin boards. This becomes a very productive building assignment and an excellent public relations (PR) program component.

Personal Commentary/Notes: _____

_____

Collect Course Selection Data *

Although the middle school electives program is not as complex as the high school's, counselors should take into account each student's interests and achievement level when preparing his or her future schedule. For our eighth graders, this is not a time for the principal to allow group scheduling. Each child, and, if possible, the child's parents or guardians should be involved in the process.

The course selection process drives the creation of the master schedule and the staffing requests for the coming year. Accuracy and attention to detail are therefore important. The projected number of class sections helps to justify your staffing needs, and any dramatic change should be reported immediately to the central office since it certainly affects the future budget. (See Resource 24: Scheduling Timeline.)

Personal Commentary/Notes: _____

January Personnel

Finalize Staffing Needs *

As stated in the previous section, it is time to make your recommendations for next year's staffing. This is based on student course requests, curriculum needs, and individual and group test results.

Middle school principals should begin to consider the personnel makeup for each team. Sometimes we have to dissolve an excellent team when we need the talent elsewhere. If teachers are told the honest reasons for the change, they'll understand it was done to balance team strength. Anything but the truth will be seen as uncaring administrative manipulation.

Personal Commentary/Notes: _____

Send Superintendent All First-Semester Teacher Evaluations *

Principals are required to collect all evaluations from their supervisory staff, add their own to the mix, and submit the evaluations to the appropriate central office administrator. Teachers with problems should receive special attention. It is strongly advised that the principal have a conference with central office personnel to discuss improvement plans for those teachers functioning below par and to review contractual language if the teacher is to be dismissed. Adherence to district policy, state law, and the teachers' contract is imperative. If not, you may open the district to a legal challenge.

Personal Commentary/Notes: _____

_____

✳ *Conduct Evaluations for Nonprofessional Staff*

Secretaries, aides, teaching assistants, and cafeteria workers deserve our opinion about their performance. Many are protected by civil service laws and have a form of job security similar to tenure. If you employ security guards, they too need to be evaluated. Since some districts hire security firms, the principal's input as to the quality of their personnel is invaluable.

The nonprofessional component of the staff assists the faculty in meeting its primary mission. Their attitude, demeanor, and mannerisms affect the school's tone. Frequently, the way a secretary answers the phone conveys that the school is a caring institution. The way a custodian answers a parent's request for directions or helps a student who has lost something is an indication that the school is user-friendly. Evaluations of nonprofessional staff should not be overlooked. It's ironic that so often this topic is hardly mentioned, if at all, in administrative texts and rarely discussed in administrative courses.

Personal Commentary/Notes: _____

_____

January Checklists

January Key Tasks

Major Assignments	Date Started	Date Completed	Days on Task
Review teacher performance evaluations			
Create remedial plans for staff			
Evaluate custodial staff			
Distribute midyear report cards			
Review department and team goals			
Review curriculum initiatives			
Finalize budget requests			
Make informal class visits			
Conduct faculty meeting			
Prepare for winter examinations			

January Communications

✓	Assignment
	Conduct parent-teacher conferences
	Coordinate PTA presentation
	Prepare for board of education meeting
	Obtain feedback on school lunch program

January Planning

✔	Assignment
	Assess sixth-grade orientation program
	Review ongoing grants
	Monitor bulletin board displays
	Collect course selection data

January Personnel

✔	Finalize
	Finalize staffing needs
	Send superintendent all first-semester teacher evaluations
	Conduct evaluations for nonprofessional staff

January Calendar

MONTH: JANUARY

YEAR: _____

MONDAY	TUESDAY	WEDNESDAY	THURSDAY	FRIDAY	SATURDAY
					SATURDAY _____
					SUNDAY _____
MONDAY _____	TUESDAY _____	WEDNESDAY _____	THURSDAY _____	FRIDAY _____	SATURDAY _____
					SUNDAY _____
MONDAY _____	TUESDAY _____	WEDNESDAY _____	THURSDAY _____	FRIDAY _____	SATURDAY _____
					SUNDAY _____
MONDAY _____	TUESDAY _____	WEDNESDAY _____	THURSDAY _____	FRIDAY _____	SATURDAY _____
					SUNDAY _____
MONDAY _____	TUESDAY _____	WEDNESDAY _____	THURSDAY _____	FRIDAY _____	SATURDAY _____
					SUNDAY _____

NOTES _____

117

Chapter Eight

A problem well stated is a problem half solved.

—Charles F. Kettering

Middle schools are unique. For many teachers, February marks the start of a new set of classes. The second semester in technology, art, music, business, health, and home and careers often is September revisited. Furthermore, as many schools adopt some form of block scheduling, teachers may face an entirely new set of students and courses in the second half of the year. Knowing this, the principal must motivate both those who teach new students and those who are continuing with the same students—not an easy task.

All of the hard work and planning completed in January will prove worthwhile if the second semester opens smoothly. The number of things that have to go right is staggering:

- Are new student schedules accurate?
- Were class lists provided for every teacher?
- Are teacher classes balanced and room assignments accurate?
- Are new student schedules alphabetized and available in the main, guidance, and nurse's offices?

- Have all necessary supplies and texts been moved to the appropriate rooms?
- Were necessary changes made in teacher building assignments?

Some school districts, particularly those in cold climates, close for vacation during Presidents' Week. This saves fuel costs and allows the custodial staff to clean the building and perform some special maintenance projects. It is a plan worthy of consideration and will not affect the minimum required days of instruction.

By the end of this month, but no later than March, rehiring and tenure recommendations must be sent to the central office. The date is usually driven by teachers' contractual language; however, even if not obligated by contracts, we owe a longer period of time to those being discharged, so they can seek a new position. These decisions are crucial to the development of the budget and signify the beginning of the upcoming year's hiring process. When advertisements for next year's staff appear in February and March, the district is usually efficiently managed.

This might be a good time to review the status of all children in special education. A brief examination of every Individual Educational Program (IEP) will prevent end-of-year surprises and impartial hearings requested by unhappy parents. Finally, we want to be sure that our staff is providing a quality program for these youngsters. In the past twenty years, the special education department has expanded greatly—as have laws associated with children with special needs. Principals must constantly receive updates on these legal requirements.

To energize the faculty, we recommend sending a thank-you memo to the staff for their first-half-year's effort. An inspirational speech for the February faculty meeting should address the five months ahead. It seems as if principals are always dividing their time in the present and in anticipation of the future. As you have probably concluded, our to-do list is never totally completed. It's always a work in progress. (See Resource 25: Inspirational Memorandum.)

FEBRUARY

February Key Tasks

Evaluate the *
Second-Semester Schedule

As you start the second half of the school year, be sure to promptly review all class sizes, teaching assignments, and program changes. Some sections become either smaller or larger because of scheduling changes, new admissions, or the special education inclusion program. Work with your counselors and balance classes as soon as possible. This should be a one- or two-day process.

Principals often ask their faculty for feedback on preparation for the new semester. Their suggestions are useful and should be incorporated into the calendar.

Personal Commentary/Notes: _____

_____

* Issue Second-Quarter Report Cards

As soon as the second-quarter report cards are issued, all counselors should be reminded to follow up on their responsibilities. The guidance department should perform the following tasks:

- Send notices to every parent whose child failed a semester or ten-week class. If failing might affect graduation, the correspondence should specifically address that possibility.
- Interview every student with multiple failures in yearlong courses.
- Set up conferences for teachers when parents have questions about grades.
- Counsel every student who has received poor conduct notices.
- Meet with teams who have students who are failing or misbehaving.
- Either the counselor, nurse, or attendance officer must follow up on students with an extraordinary number of absences or lateness to school.

Many principals send messages to parents as attachments to report cards. The message might include a notice about upcoming events as well as explanations about the report cards. Reiterate the procedure parents should follow when they need to contact a guidance counselor or speak to a specific teacher. If the report card's explanations are too brief and need to be augmented, include more in-depth analysis in a letter. Mentioning the school's phone number and how important it is for lines of communication to be open throughout the year is a positive invitation to work together to help each child.

Personal Commentary/Notes: _____

_____

* Complete Evaluations of Nontenured Teachers

We discussed this issue in a previous section; however, here we offer another way to handle the dismissal process for a nontenured teacher. Give teachers the opportunity to resign rather than go through the termination process. Not having the firing on their record might help the teacher to secure a position in another district.

We stress that if any doubt about a teacher's competence remains after the three-year probationary period, we recommend dismissal. We find no fault with principals who don't rehire after the second year when a teacher hasn't shown that he or she will be a valuable addition to the staff. In our view, average simply is not good enough.

Personal Commentary/Notes: _____

_____

Plan Monthly Faculty Meeting ✳

Devote a portion of this month's faculty meeting to an evaluation of the start of the second semester. Faculty suggestions and questions should be encouraged. Remind the staff about due dates for plans for each team's culminating activity. We recommend planning activities early to avoid taking field trips after early May.

Hopefully, there will be some substantive issues to discuss. This might be the time to explore which summer writing projects should be requested and list them in order of importance. In this way, the staff members always have their most important needs included in the budget. If a memo can cover the topics of the meeting, cancel the meeting.

Personal Commentary/Notes: _____

_____

Meet With Key Personnel ✳
About Next Year's Master Schedule

A well-conceived master schedule provides both students and staff with the best possible schedule. Extensive preparation and planning is necessary to make this a reality. In February, begin working with key personnel to develop the upcoming schedule.

Many middle school principals distribute a form requesting each teacher's preference for team assignment. If there are staff members with whom they'd like to work, their names should be noted. If there is trust between teachers and the principal, teachers will also mention those faculty members with whom they'd prefer not to be teamed. Often, teachers like either a heavy morning or a heavy afternoon class schedule. Such requests can be accommodated when starting the schedule early.

One word about room assignments is in order. Whenever possible, give as many teachers their own classrooms. This promotes ownership. The furniture, bulletin boards, and the entire atmosphere will reflect the teacher's pride. When rooms are shared, neither faculty member claims responsibility for the physical environment. If overcrowding is an issue, this option may not be possible but remains a goal when developing the room assignment schedule.

Personal Commentary/Notes: _____

_____

* *Review Teacher and Departmental Grades*

After every distribution of report cards, grades should be examined by supervisors to identify obvious areas of concern. Discussions should be held with teachers who have atypical grade distributions. All new staff members should have discussions about their grades prior to submitting them for input on the report cards. This is a suggested item for your new teacher orientation program and a demand for your supervisors to fulfill.

Personal Commentary/Notes: _____

_____

* *Host a Career Fair*

Though we are aware that even ninth and tenth graders usually have unrealistic career aspirations, we urge an annual career day program. Middle school students should be exposed to the many opportunities they will have in the world of work. No pressure on decisions should be made at this age. However, exploring career clusters is highly recommended by middle school theorists. For example, a student thinking about being a physician should also take note of other scientific careers, such as nursing, physiotherapy, podiatry, and optometry. Encourage students to think in terms of broad areas of interest and not be concerned about narrowing their options.

Having a student's parent participate in career day is an example of school-home cooperation. The community aspect is expanded more by the representation of the members of local service organizations. Teachers representing the field of education are usually inundated by student questions. Keeping a list of people who have volunteered to represent their occupation helps to develop the following year's invitation list. If the event can be coordinated with assignments required in the home and careers course, it will be truly curriculum related.

Personal Commentary/Notes: _____

_____

* *Plan for Eighth-Grade Graduation*

Most middle schools have abandoned formal eighth-grade graduations in favor of a moving-up exercise. Many schools continue to schedule some end-of-year grade-level activity. Some fond farewell activities are recommended as an appropriate end to the students' middle school experience. If planning begins at this time, unique and poignant events can be planned. For example, at one school, we noticed poems about each student as part of the decorations in the gym at a school dance. The poems were written on the shape of a heart or the school's emblem, and when students left the dance, they were allowed to take the poems for souvenirs. The parents and teachers who organized the event took the time to write a personal poetic tribute to every child. Years later, many parents reported that their children still had their poems displayed in their rooms. This is another example of why middle schools are so special.

Personal Commentary/Notes: _____

_____

February Communications

Prepare Board of * *Education Report*

This report is an opportunity to present some of the middle school's critical needs as part of the budget highlights. If the principal can demonstrate how his or her budget requests will help student performance, the requested items have a good chance of being in the next year's budget. Involving students in such meetings is another technique to gain the attention of board members. Middle school principals must not allow the larger number of high school requests to dominate the meeting. Be sure to include the superintendent's advice and get his or her consent prior to making your presentation to the board.

Personal Commentary/Notes: _____

_____

Request Congratulatory Letters From Elected Officials *

Just as we request letters from public officials for retiring staff members, we also ask them to write letters of congratulations to our graduates. These letters make a great addition to any program's handout or playbill. It is also a valuable public relations (PR) component.

Personal Commentary/Notes: _____

_____

Hold Midyear Conferences *

Meet with team leaders and departmental supervisors to develop and review the end-of-year culminating activities. These activities—field days, science fairs, art shows, and field trips—must not conflict with testing schedules or other high-profile events. If additional supervision is needed for the activities, ask parents to serve as chaperones. If the teacher contract provides for paid faculty to provide supervision, these estimated costs should come from a budget line titled "Audience Control."

Other midyear conferences serve the following functions:

- Remind principals to check the budget and review expenditures to ensure supply codes are sufficient to meet expenses for the remainder of the year
- Help curriculum leaders to finalize summer curriculum projects
- Allow teachers to review new state mandates to ensure any realignment of a topic is covered in the approved curriculum
- Inform counselors about how many children are in danger of not getting promoted

Retention remains a middle school issue, but most districts are requiring a summer program for students who fail two or more full-year courses. Every member of the staff should be made aware of your board of education's policy on promotion and retention.

Personal Commentary/Notes: _____

_____

* Prepare PTA Presentation

Develop a calendar for parents that denotes every end-of-year activity. Walk them through each event, explaining its purpose and educational value. Ask for volunteers to serve as a support system for teachers who may have requested assistance during their midyear conferences.

If you want to maximize support for your budget proposals, make a complete presentation at the February or March PTA meeting. Building improvements and equipment acquisition geared to helping students reach their proper assessment levels will be endorsed by parents. If parents clearly understand why requests for material, supplies, and textbooks are being made, they will be better able to serve as a support system to articulate your cause. A unified school and community can be very influential at a school board's decision-making session.

Personal Commentary/Notes: _____

_____

* Encourage Teachers to Schedule Parent Conferences

Encourage teachers to call or schedule conferences with parents of students who are doing poorly, who are not behaving well, or whose work habits have suddenly changed. These meetings usually help to avoid less-pleasant conferences in June. Positive changes should be reported as well because these accolades are very much appreciated by parents and serve to motivate students to try harder. As stated earlier, this is prime time for your counseling department to assist teachers. Don't let the scheduling process for next year consume all of the counselors' time. Counselors should be meeting with their teams to help call parents whose children are slacking off or failing.

Personal Commentary/Notes: _____

_____

Compose Honor Roll Congratulatory Letters *

Many middle schools presently publish two levels of academic achievement. One is simply referred to as the honor roll and the second is called the high honor roll. Principals' secretaries mail a personal congratulatory letter to every student whose name appears on the honor rolls. The principal merely affixes his or her signature and may or may not add a personal note. It's easily done and makes for great PR.

A good middle school should also have a way to acknowledge students whose work is improving. Honoring a student of the month is another method that has gained popularity. Teams, subject departments, and special education teachers may submit their students for this recognition. Local newspapers often print the student's picture with a brief article about his or her accomplishments. This validates the school's caring environment.

Personal Commentary/Notes: _____

_____

February Planning

Meet With High School *
Counselors

This could just as well be listed under key tasks, but since it's organized by the high school staff, we view it as planning for our graduating class. In preparation for the transition to the high school, both high school and middle school principals and their guidance personnel should meet to do the following:

- Provide middle-level counselors an orientation about current high school course offerings.
- Inform the middle-level staff about the criteria for placement in each course or level.
- Plan for the high school counselors to make a presentation at the middle school. The high school chairpersons and student leaders should be part of this presentation.
- Review how the present ninth grade is doing in the high school to give feedback to the middle-level staff.
- Review the entire orientation program.
- Enter all dates related to this process on the middle school calendar to avoid conflicts.

Personal Commentary/Notes: _____

_____

* Check on Status of School Supplies

Just as we consistently check the budget for money that has not yet been expended, supplies must be checked on a regular basis to prevent shortages from developing. Care must be taken with ten-week courses and semester courses to guarantee that students have the same amount of materials as did the children enrolled earlier in the year. Efficient record keeping will make the yearly budget request for supplies easier to justify.

Many school districts are making purchases in bulk by joining educational cooperatives, which lowers costs. The disadvantages, however, are that ordering times may not suit your district, and a different brand of merchandise is often substituted for what your teachers ordered.

Personal Commentary/Notes: _____

_____

* Establish Due Dates for Chairpersons' Scheduling Input

Staff, assistant principals, and department supervisors play a key role in determining student and teacher schedules. We touched on getting staff preferences for team assignments. Now is the time to develop next year's student programs. Forms used to enter data into a computer must be designed, and a training session for counselors should be arranged. Many principals who have small schools prefer to create schedules by hand. If they know the students, it's easy to avoid placing two children who may be incompatible in the same class or team. The problems with scheduling by hand are that schedules and class lists often take a long time to assemble, and making changes at a later time can be overwhelming. With today's technology, hand scheduling is simply too labor intensive. Counselors should have a way to separate students who don't belong together.

Many eighth graders now take high school courses, and a means to set criteria and make recommendations for their placement in such accelerated courses must be developed for the middle school counselor. Parents often want their children placed in advanced courses. Establish specific requirements to help avoid issues of rejection when parents, students, and counselors hold their scheduling meetings. If there is a gifted program, entrance requirements must be well publicized and adhered to at all times.

Personal Commentary/Notes: _____

_____

Coordinate Preparation of ✱ *Facilities and Grounds for Spring*

With the arrival of spring just around the corner, it is time to meet with the director of buildings and grounds and your head custodian to plan for the start of outdoor activities. These staff members should furnish the principal with an ongoing system of field maintenance to ensure that children have a safe place to play. The grounds must be checked daily because community children use them after school hours and on weekends. An early-morning job for a building custodian should include an inspection of such areas as playgrounds, fields, and tennis courts, and all broken bottles and debris should be removed immediately. For our northern state principals, this planning session could occur a month or two later.

Personal Commentary/Notes: _____

_____

February Personnel

Evaluate New Teacher ✱ *Orientation Program*

We have talked about assessing the new teacher orientation program. This evaluation should be completed and readied for the following year. Remember to file it in two places: the first in the August file and the second in the file marked "New Teacher Orientation."

Personal Commentary/Notes: _____

_____

* *Develop a Dialogue With Support Staff*

Although principals have already evaluated support staff, they should meet with them regularly to secure their suggestions. Often, secretaries have ideas that help make the office function more efficiently. A brief regularly scheduled meeting can reap many benefits and make everyone feel part of the staff.

The same benefit can be derived from meeting with custodians. These men and women often know what's going on in the halls and know the students who are problematic. They help to keep the building secure and often inform staff members about areas that have a potential for trouble. They usually live in the community and are a valuable source of information. Their suggestions should be encouraged and acted on when appropriate.

Personal Commentary/Notes: _____

_____

February Checklists

February Key Tasks

Major Assignments	Date Started	Date Completed	Days on Task
Evaluate the second-semester schedule			
Issue second-quarter report cards			
Complete evaluations of nontenured teachers			
Plan monthly faculty meeting			
Meet with key personnel about next year's master schedule			
Review teacher and departmental grades			
Host a career fair			
Plan for eighth-grade graduation			

February Communications

✓	Assignment
	Prepare board of education report
	Request congratulatory letters from elected officials
	Hold midyear conferences
	Prepare PTA presentation
	Encourage teachers to schedule parent conferences
	Compose honor roll congratulatory letters

February Planning

✓	Assignment
	Meet with high school counselors
	Check on status of school supplies
	Establish due dates for chairperson's scheduling input
	Coordinate preparation of facilities and grounds for spring

February Personnel

✓	Finalize
	Evaluate new teacher orientation program
	Develop a dialogue with support staff

February Calendar

MONTH: FEBRUARY

YEAR: _____

MONDAY	TUESDAY	WEDNESDAY	THURSDAY	FRIDAY	SATURDAY
					SUNDAY
MONDAY	TUESDAY	WEDNESDAY	THURSDAY	FRIDAY	SATURDAY
					SUNDAY
MONDAY	TUESDAY	WEDNESDAY	THURSDAY	FRIDAY	SATURDAY
					SUNDAY
MONDAY	TUESDAY	WEDNESDAY	THURSDAY	FRIDAY	SATURDAY
					SUNDAY
MONDAY	TUESDAY	WEDNESDAY	THURSDAY	FRIDAY	SATURDAY
					SUNDAY

NOTES

_____

131

Chapter Nine

The secret of education lies in respecting the pupil.

—Ralph Waldo Emerson

March is usually free of national holidays and thus has a full calendar of twenty-one to twenty-three school days. In April, we have spring recess, and in May, we have the Memorial Day weekend. June is an abbreviated month because of the start of the summer vacation. March is thus a month of intense school and a period in which the creative administrator must balance education and culminating plans.

Staff can generate interest in the middle school's daily program by holding some special events. The events should be designed to meet major curriculum objectives. Activities such as a science fair, an art and technology exhibit, a multicultural event, a career day, or a mathematics olympiad can be organized to remotivate the children and the staff as well. The excitement often carries over to the classroom during these dark and short winter days.

Teacher shortages, especially in mathematics and science, require attention to both the rehiring process and the district's interviewing procedures. We strongly recommend that principals complete the supervision of new teachers and make decisions as early as possible about retention or termination of employment. This enables the district to advertise in March and April, which gives administrators more time to select the best available candidates for the following year. If principals don't view this as a competitive situation, they are doomed to interview teachers who have been rejected by adjoining districts. If you peruse the teacher want ads in June, July, and August, you can readily identify the districts with inferior hiring practices.

Remind staff that the end of the third marking period is rapidly approaching. The March interim report is second in importance to the final one, which will be sent in May. Teachers and counselors must bring to the attention of their immediate supervisors the names of all students who may fail a course. If possible, special tutoring should be arranged or recommended to parents. Most staff members provide extra help for students before or after school. Teachers should inform students of this service, and it should be announced over the public address system on a weekly basis.

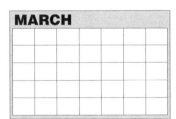

March Key Tasks

Prepare to Defend *
Budget Requests

Although the principal must be the advocate for middle school budget proposals, efforts to identify the needs of the building must be a group activity. Details for each request must be researched, and the principal has sole responsibility for articulating them clearly. For example, if the science department has requested a classroom set of new microscopes, the principal should do the following:

1. Document the current number of outdated or broken microscopes.

2. Discuss how new microscopes will help the science staff to successfully complete a specific state curriculum requirement.

3. Produce specific costs from several vendors.

4. Present warranty information.

These tasks can be accomplished only if the principal is kept informed by the appropriate staff experts. Each curriculum area supervisor knows more about his or her subject's specific needs than the principal does. By including supervisors' input, the successful defense of your school's budget is truly a team effort.

Personal Commentary/Notes: _____
_____

✻ *Continue Work on Master Schedule*

Continue your work on the development of next year's master schedule. If the counselors have completed scheduling one grade level, start experimenting with the data. By meeting frequently with other building supervisors, you can become apprised of their wish list concerning the schedule. Some questions about the schedule, such as the following, will need to be addressed: Is there a way to schedule double periods for science labs? Is it possible to do the same for home and careers classes, so students can actually prepare, cook, and eat a meal in an extended class period?

Another meeting with counselors could make you aware of some of their programming problems from the previous year. For example, if a large chorus class is scheduled for Monday, Wednesday, and Friday, it's difficult to schedule another large group of children on Tuesday and Thursday. Counselors and deans may have strong opinions about whether lunches should be scheduled to separate or integrate grade levels. On a more personal level, principals need to consider which teachers seem to be effective with the most able students and which seem to be more effective with the academically challenged students. Along those lines, principals should give thought to particularly difficult children, scheduling them with the best disciplinarians. These are all important considerations a principal must confront when developing a master schedule, and the wise principal solicits help from all staff members so the best possible schedule is created.

It might be too early to discuss the makeup of teacher teams. However, most principals begin formulating their ideas. Finalizing the process may have to wait until new faculty members are hired. Principals confess that the construction of their teams occupies their thoughts throughout the school year.

Personal Commentary/Notes: _____

_____

✻ *Prepare for Summer School Program*

Shockingly, there are districts that don't involve the middle school principal in the hiring process for the summer school principal and assistant principal. This can only be called an institutional sin. The regular middle school principal should provide the summer school administration with a complete orientation, which includes, but is not be limited to, the following topics:

1. The curriculum that will be offered

2. Grading procedures and the date by which final grades should be submitted to the middle school guidance counselors (guidance counselors should have time to make necessary changes in class assignments before the start of the regular school year)

3. Equipment that can or cannot be used in the summer school

4. Rooms that are to remain secure

5. Disciplinary expectations

6. Respect for the facility

7. Custodial and maintenance projects in progress during the summer

8. Operating procedures concerning the use of the public address system, the fire alarm system, the clock system, and so forth

Courses offered should be primarily academic in nature. Expanded art and music programs need special funding and board approval. The development of standards-based education and accountability mandates will most likely expand the responsibilities of the middle school summer program and will require thoughtful planning by all concerned.

Personal Commentary/Notes: _____

_____

Finalize Summer Writing Projects *

Most districts now give priority to summer curriculum-writing projects to accommodate specific changes in state mandates. For example, if social studies requirements change, the school district must revise its curriculum for that subject, and social studies becomes the top funding priority. Most subject supervisors are frequently in contact with their state department leaders to keep up-to-date. By March or April, district leaders should know every new state mandate.

Poorer districts have greater difficulty in adjusting to the sudden changes in mandates. Enrichment activities, the arts, and all nonmandated changes rarely receive summer funding. Of late, parents have been asked to pay higher fees for enrichment activities, such as foreign language immersion programs, music lessons, and summer camps. Districts that have a solid tax base can offer more educational opportunities because they do not rely as much on federal funding as poorer districts. Educational funding has gotten tighter across the nation since the September 11, 2001, attacks and the prioritization of homeland security.

Personal Commentary/Notes: _____

_____

Complete All Teacher Evaluations *

Using the evaluation process correctly is as important as an evaluation's write-up. Make sure that each staff member has received all required documentation in writing. Evaluations should be signed by both the principal and the teacher. When controversy arises, a statement saying that the teacher has read the evaluation but disagrees with the assessment should be signed. If the teacher wants a union or building representative to sit in on the postobservation conference, a second administrator should also be present. District attorneys should be called on by the superintendent to assist the principal during any evaluation that becomes controversial.

Evaluations must meet the following criteria:

1. Conform to education law

2. Be consistent with the teachers' union contract

3. Be part of the district's evaluation program

4. Be written in such a way as to stress the need to improve instruction

5. Document every area in which an administrator has noted unsatisfactory performance

Personal Commentary/Notes: _____

_____

* Begin to Organize School Recognition Program

There are both state and national middle school recognition programs. Applications for this recognition require progress reports, and the process is often its own reward since the entire faculty must ultimately get involved. The self-examination required by your staff and the scrutiny of the programs will be beneficial whether you win recognition or not. Check with your superintendent prior to broaching the subject with your staff in the event the district does not want competition between schools.

There are also middle school state recognition programs, from which many benefits are derived. Site visits by teachers and administrators from outside your district evaluate every aspect of your school, including the school's statistics, academic tone, and general environment. Their subsequent report provides excellent goals for the following year. Staff members interested in school improvement challenges can make applications to be reviewed by these objective professionals.

Personal Commentary/Notes: _____

_____

* Conduct Faculty Meeting

Several substantive tasks are on March's agenda, and faculty participation is recommended. A meeting to review the past student orientation program garners suggestions from every department. Asking for people to serve on a committee to redesign the orientation effort is certainly appropriate. Staff members interested in administration and those superior teachers who have been serving as mentors make excellent committee members. Naturally, your counselors should be included since they often implement much of the orientation phases.

Rather than making a unilateral decision, principals should ask the faculty if they want to participate in Middle-Level Education Month, which is celebrated in March. One of the planned monthly programs could be dedicated to the middle school concept. If a department or team would like to sponsor the event, they can volunteer at the open meeting. Naturally, the principal might offer some suggestions, but following the faculty's wishes would reassure faculty that they are part of the decision-making process.

This is also a good time to select faculty members who will be involved in the hiring of new teachers. Once the committees are formed, some inservice training should be provided. These staff members must be made aware of questions that are illegal to ask in an interview. Also, the conduct of the interview should be reviewed and the exact questions to ask of the candidates should be determined. Some sample questions for teacher candidates are included in the resources. (See Resource 26: Interview Questions for Teachers.)

Personal Commentary/Notes: _____

_____

March Communications

Set Meeting Dates *
With Elementary Principals

The start of the middle school orientation program for present fifth graders begins in two months. Therefore, write a letter to each elementary principal reserving dates for your counselors to visit their schools. Many states have inaugurated standardized testing at the elementary level, and these tests are administered in the spring of each year. Knowing this, our staff must work around the elementary schools' testing schedule. Most elementary school teachers do not want the orientation to begin earlier than late May because they feel fifth graders will think the year is over and quit studying. Although the meetings for parents and students occur in late May or early June, the process starts now.

Typically, counselors visit each class and present a detailed orientation about the middle school. Later, a meeting is held with each elementary teacher to learn more about each child. At this time, the special needs of youngsters are discussed and the names of children who should not be placed in the same class are relayed to those doing the schedule. We detail the entire process in May, which is when the visits occur, but the first communication has to be initiated now.

Personal Commentary/Notes: _____

_____

* Supervise Closing Activities

The end of the year is one of the busiest times for student activities and programs. Many faculty members are needed to supervise the events. If these teachers are given extra pay for this work, the principal should give everyone an opportunity to serve. Most teacher contracts specify that these assignments should be distributed in an equitable manner. In this case, principals find they are unable to hire the most competent supervisor because the contract forces them to offer the position to the next teacher on the list.

Hiring supervisors can become a burden since principals must ensure that every activity is adequately staffed. This is why principals rarely miss an end-of-year school function. As one principal said, "If I'm responsible for the safety of the kids, I'm not delegating the supervision to anyone else!"

Personal Commentary/Notes: _____

_____

* Plan Monthly Board of Education Presentation

Some principals feel that these meetings, month after month, are burdensome. Though they are time-consuming, it is your responsibility to properly represent your middle school staff and students. One principal from Maryland presents her school's test data in March. She augments her delivery with a polished, computer-generated presentation, with clear and comprehensive tables and graphs. The results are shared, and summary materials are distributed to everyone in attendance. She then adroitly ties the results to the need for summer school or summer curriculum projects. Any poor score comes with a prescription of how her staff members feel their statistics can be improved. She further informs the public that her staff is conducting an item analysis to determine if the questions answered incorrectly were part of the district's curriculum. If they were not, a summer writing project is recommended. If the subject matter related to the incorrect responses were part of the district's curriculum, a workshop is held to explore how the topic should be taught better. This is a perfect example of how to turn a negative into a positive.

Personal Commentary/Notes: _____

_____

Prepare PTA Meeting Presentation *

The following list is presented to help keep the PTA's topics worthwhile and relevant:

1. Discuss plans for the PTA's final annual function. Establish committees to be responsible for coordinating the event.

2. Consider possibilities for the annual end-of-year gift to the school.

3. Review other projects that the PTA has funded.

4. Explore how parents can best be involved in the school's closing activities.

5. Discuss how the PTA will support the principal's presentation to the board concerning test scores and curriculum-writing projects.

6. Develop a plan to encourage voter participation on the upcoming school budget.

Never forget that the members of the PTA form the basis of your support system. Making them feel a part of your administration encourages more effort on their part. These are your yes votes on budgets, bond issues, and middle school funding requests. We never recommend preferential treatment for PTA members.

Personal Commentary/Notes: _____

_____

March Planning

Conduct *
Statewide Examinations

In many states, courses culminate with formal examinations developed by committees at the state's education department. In New York, students taking eighth-grade advanced courses in mathematics must take the State of New York Regent's Examination. The tests are ordered in March and must remain secured in safes or locked storage closets. The test is administered at an exact time in all middle schools throughout the state. This trend of testing and accountability is growing throughout the nation, even though these formalities are more typical of high school testing.

Other formal statewide examinations to measure achievement in mathematics, English, and reading are becoming more commonplace. Planning by the principal requires the following:

- Submitting orders for the correct number of test papers from the state
- Informing teachers about the dates and making sure there are no calendar conflicts
- Making sure that teacher lesson plans indicate appropriate review for the tests
- Having subject supervisors review the curriculum to be certain the district's course outlines cover the specific test material
- Explaining the purpose of the tests to teachers, students, and parents

Personal Commentary/Notes: _____

_____

* Begin Summer School Preparations

We've stated rather strongly that the middle school principal should be involved in the selection of the summer school administrators. Time should be taken in the next two months to decide the courses to be offered. Principals usually arrange a meeting with the middle school guidance counselors, who by now have a good idea of the number of potential failures in each subject.

If the district will fund enrichment activities during the summer, staff members should be asked for their suggestions. Some middle school students have been academically motivated by attending summer courses in drama, music theory, and not-for-credit individualized projects. A principal reported that during one summer session, a student constructed eight musical instruments, another painted a twenty-foot mural on the gymnasium wall, and another designed and replicated a colonial village using only clay and twigs. Releasing student creativity is a good investment.

Personal Commentary/Notes: _____

_____

* Begin Planning for Annual Awards Assembly

A faculty committee should be appointed to review all awards given in June as well as the criteria for each award. One sensitive topic involves the naming of awards in honor of people. Inevitably, the time comes when the person whose name is on the award is no longer known by the present student body. When this happens, the faculty committee typically debates whether to keep the name or to replace it with another, more well-known name. The debate can get heated and result in hard feelings. To avoid this dilemma, the awards committee would be wise to decide the number of years the award will be offered when it is first established. Developing procedures that eliminate foreseeable problems is a laudable administrative skill.

We urge a balance between academic, citizenship, improvement, and outstanding effort awards. Remind the staff that the latter categories merit recognition and are part of our middle school philosophy.

Personal Commentary/Notes: _____

_____

March Personnel

Begin New ＊
Teacher Hiring Process

Begin the new teacher hiring process as soon as possible. Advertising at local colleges and in newspapers and educational journals helps to increase the pool of candidates. Conduct an initial screening to ensure all candidates have the proper certification. Then, send the applications to the school's interview committee. The committee should develop questions to be asked of all candidates. Prior to interviewing, candidates should be asked to give a writing sample for review at a later time.

Starting early makes it possible to avoid any rush to judgment. Student teachers who worked in the building should be given an opportunity to interview. As with all who are hired, the superintendent must make the final recommendation, and the board must vote its approval for the candidate to become a member of the staff.

Don't forget to call the applicant's references. Even though these people are selected by the candidate, their enthusiasm, or lack of it, may give you valuable information about the candidate's abilities and potential.

Personal Commentary/Notes: _____

Send Reminder Notes to Supervisory Staff ＊

Sending personal reminders to the supervisory staff about the numerous requirements during the remaining few months are usually helpful and appreciated. Notes might remind supervisors to do the following:

- Submit final recommendations for summer curriculum projects.
- Adhere to due dates for duplication of finals.
- Provide appropriate security for final examination tests.
- Complete all nontenured teacher evaluations.
- Prepare for upcoming quarterly report cards.
- Select department award recipients.

Personal Commentary/Notes: _____

_____

March Checklists

March Key Tasks

Major Assignments	Date Started	Date Completed	Days on Task
Prepare to defend budget requests			
Continue work on master schedule			
Prepare for summer school program			
Finalize summer writing projects			
Complete all teacher evaluations			
Begin to organize school recognition program			
Conduct faculty meeting			

March Communications

✓	Assignment
	Set meeting dates with elementary principals
	Supervise closing activities
	Plan monthly board of education presentation
	Prepare PTA meeting presentation

March Planning

✓	Assignment
	Conduct statewide examinations
	Begin summer school preparations
	Begin planning for annual awards assembly

March Personnel

✓	Finalize
	Begin new teacher hiring process
	Send reminder notes to supervisory staff

March Calendar

MONTH: MARCH

YEAR: ____

MONDAY	TUESDAY	WEDNESDAY	THURSDAY	FRIDAY	SATURDAY
____	____	____	____	____	SATURDAY ____
					SUNDAY ____
____	____	____	____	____	SATURDAY ____
					SUNDAY ____
____	____	____	____	____	SATURDAY ____
					SUNDAY ____
____	____	____	____	____	SATURDAY ____
					SUNDAY ____
____	____	____	____	____	SATURDAY ____
					SUNDAY ____

NOTES

_____

145

Chapter Ten

Excellence . . . is not an act, but a habit.

—Aristotle

hird-quarter report cards are sent home this month. The work of the guidance department is most critical at this time. Next year's scheduling demands should not detract from the counseling process. Principals should make a list of all students who are in danger of failing for the year. Every counselor should initial the list after counseling each child and informing his or her parent or guardian. If this sounds a bit rigid, we plead guilty. "No surprises" is one of our mottoes. Parents, student tutors, and teachers should all be aware of the importance of the last ten weeks of school. We will feel no discomfort when we repeat this sentiment after the last interim report in May.

By this time of the year, many student clubs and organizations are beginning to wind down their activities. The importance of these clubs and the impact that their advisors can have on the students should not be underestimated. In many ways, students' involvement in clubs is just as important as their work on a classroom assignment. Regrettably, however, some principals neglect to properly assess the effectiveness of club advisors. We feel that their selection should be carefully considered, and selection should not be made on the basis of seniority. A good advisor is capable of accomplishing many of the functions of a good counselor. In the informal setting of a club, students frequently are more open in expressing their personal and family concerns. Therefore, advisors should be reappointed only if they are competent and can maintain their enthusiasm and creativity. When evaluating a club advisor, principals should have them put in writing their accomplishments for the year. This information helps the principal make a fair and objective evaluation of the advisor's performance.

By April, the middle school budget is now out of your hands. It is being reviewed by central office personnel, the superintendent, and the board of education. If the principal was thorough in preparing the school's requests, every group of requested items will be presented in priority order. Sometimes the superintendent has to cut some budgetary requests during the final meeting with the board, and it is important that the cuts be made from the least-critical requests. Finally, if offered a last opportunity to present your budget to the board of education, your performance should be well rehearsed and given with passion and confidence.

Some consideration should be given to redesigning your new teacher orientation program. By now, you have received the requested feedback from your staff. Meet with a small committee and itemize each component that was deemed successful. Now, file the information in your August file and duplicate it for the new teacher evaluation folder.

The planning for the new student orientation should have been completed in March. This month, you must decide, with the elementary principals and your counselors, when to have the first evening meeting with parents of fifth graders. Any evening in April or May seems appropriate as long as it does not present a conflict for other schools in the district.

Don't forget that the April vacation period affords you another opportunity to meet with your custodial staff and plan cleaning and maintenance tasks. Head custodians should submit their proposals prior to the vacation and submit their accomplishments when vacation is over. Going beyond minimal expectations is an objective for head custodians and should be a standard on their evaluations.

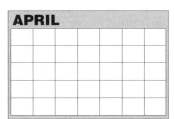

April Key Tasks

Complete Master Schedule *
for Coming Year

As stated in the introduction to this chapter, the master schedule should be nearing completion. Some assignments may await the hiring process. We urge principals not to give new teachers the most difficult assignments and the poorest room assignments. Try to build success rather than frustration.

Take the time to carefully look at each teacher's schedule, particularly if an assistant principal has done most of the process. Teachers should not have a schedule with three classes, followed by a building assignment and then another class. Use lunch and preparation periods to break up several consecutive teaching assignments. Staff attitudes about administrators are often formed from such considerations. If we say we care, our practice should demonstrate that principle.

Personal Commentary/Notes: _____

_____

* Conduct New Student Orientation for Fifth Graders

By now, the principal has probably started to receive calls from anxious elementary school parents. This is normal and should not be upsetting. Answer the calls cordially since this is your first contact with these parents, who might be insecure. Telling them about the scheduled parent meeting alleviates many concerns. Having a child enter middle school can be traumatic for parents. Their children are leaving the comfort of a small school, which they've attended for six years, if we include kindergarten. Both parents and children are probably known by name to the elementary building principal and most of the staff. To help avoid insecurities, we host both a student and parent orientation program.

When writing the first letter home to your prospective parents of sixth graders, be sure to include a word or two about the middle school program and philosophy. Knowledge about the school's program can help calm nervous moms and dads. A brief discussion about how teams and advisories help the professional staff get to know their children is also welcomed. This is the time for the principal to be proactive and demonstrate compassion and understanding of parents' apprehensions.

Personal Commentary/Notes: _____

_____

* Participate in Orientation for Eighth Graders

Remember, we have children entering and leaving the middle school. Many middle school principals help their counterparts in the high school to kick off their orientation program. They do this by hosting a parents' coffee hour at the middle school and inviting the high school principal for a question-and-answer session. Coupling this activity with your monthly PTA meeting is practical at this time of the year.

Just as the elementary principal is dealing with the anxiety of parents of fifth graders, the middle school principal must ease the tensions of the eighth graders' parents. Principals want parents to feel the middle school staff cares deeply about their children's adjustment to the high school. It may not be a written component of your public relations program, but it should be evidenced by your professional practice.

Personal Commentary/Notes: _____

_____

Make Public Presentation on Proposed Budget ✻

Principals have an obligation to present their final budgetary requests to their parents. Highlights of new programs and their cost factors should be explained. If creative budgeting has saved the residents money, that too should be highlighted. Provide members of the audience with understandable one-page handouts. Remember, parents generally vote in support of the school budget. In talking to their neighbors, parents should be able to articulate many reasons why their neighbors should vote for your budget.

Personal Commentary/Notes: _____

_____

Conduct Election for ✻
Student Government Officers

Present sixth- and seventh-grade students are usually ready to vote for the following year's class officers in April or May. Organize the procedures and select the date with the class advisors. Again, make sure to avoid conflicts with other events. (That's why the school calendar is a living document.)

The incoming class is not a concern at this time. We allow them one to three months to get to know each other before they vote for their class officers. Tentatively reserve next October as the date for sixth graders to vote for their student officers and student council representatives.

Not everyone can be a winner of an election. Principals should recognize and applaud those who have the courage and motivation to run for office. (See Resource 27: Sample Letter Sent to All Those Running for School Offices.)

Personal Commentary/Notes: _____

_____

Initiate Student Awards Selection Process ✻

As soon as third-quarter grades are official, discussions about academic awards should begin. We suggest that each department hold a meeting to select departmental award nominees. At a later date, a faculty meeting can be called to confirm these nominees. First, vote on all of the nondepartmental awards, and then permit the faculty members to make comments about proposed recipients of departmental awards. Sometimes a superior academic student has some serious character flaws. Faculty consensus is difficult to achieve, so prepare for a spirited meeting.

Middle school principals usually separate the awards/recognition assembly from the moving-up exercises. This is done to limit the length of both assemblies and the desire to treat all children equally at the moving-up program. There are usually three student speakers at the awards assembly: the student council president, the valedictorian, and the salutatorian.

Personal Commentary/Notes: _____

_____

* *Review Quarterly Report Cards*

Third-quarter report cards enable counselors, teachers, and administrators to identify students having serious academic difficulty. We stated that the communication of these student names is the responsibility of the entire staff. Board policies and state mandates generally determine promotional requirements. More middle schools are beginning to reflect a high school attitude about course failures. Summer school is often required if more than one forty-week course is failed. Retention is also a possibility. The entire staff should know the board policy on promotion and retention. Principals must address this in one of their spring faculty meetings and in a weekly memo to staff.

Several times in previous chapters we mentioned the awesome responsibility of the counseling staff after the mailing of interim reports and report cards. There is no room for error if we want to guarantee there will be no unpleasant surprises for our parents. To avoid a child slipping through the cracks, the principal should keep a list of all children who may fail. The counselors are required to initial the list, affirming that contact was made with each parent and child, informing them of the consequences they face if the child's work doesn't improve over the last ten weeks. Parents who complain that they were not informed about their child's poor work should be presented with the signed notification. It's not simply a matter of covering oneself—it's doing the job properly.

Personal Commentary/Notes: _____

_____

April Communications

* *Make PTA Presentation*

We cannot overstate how important it is to get the PTA behind the district's budgetary efforts. At the April PTA meeting, we make it a point to highlight several aspects of the budget. We start by distributing a prepared handout that contains not only the middle school requests but also the specific reasons the items are needed. We also remind parents of the date, time, and place for voting. If there are candidates running for board seats, we mention their names but never take sides. Remember, we have to work with any candidate who gets elected.

Furthermore, we like to invite the high school principal to this meeting to review the orientation program for eighth-grade students. This is usually a well-attended and informative meeting. It's also the first opportunity for your most active parents to meet the high school principal.

Personal Commentary/Notes: _____

_____

Attend Monthly Board of Education Meeting *

To keep the board and community informed about middle school issues, the principal might give a presentation on one of the following topics:

- A five-year study of middle school test scores

- How summer curriculum-writing projects are used to improve the curriculum and test scores

- The cooperation between the high school and the middle school, and the elementary school and the middle school, as demonstrated by the fifth- and eighth-grade orientation programs

Personal Commentary/Notes: _____

_____

Send Congratulatory Letter to Honor Roll Students *

Send out laudatory letters to students who did well or showed improvement on the third-quarter report cards. Some schools provide a special breakfast for these students on a predetermined day, calling it Student Recognition Day.

Personal Commentary/Notes: _____

_____

Establish Parameters for Spring Musical *

The preparation and staging of a schoolwide musical play takes months of work for the staff and students. Potential for conflict with testing dates and culminating activities exists, so be sure the calendar is checked. A meeting should be held to review all parameters for rehearsals, to set construction, and to set dates for the in-school and evening shows. Due to the impact of increasing test days and team field trips, many middle schools are eliminating the spring play.

Personal Commentary/Notes: _____

_____

* Complete Faculty Evaluations

All faculty evaluations should be completed this month. It's possible to do a few in May for your excellent staff members, but every critical evaluation should be completed and passed along to the central office. May and June should be a time to give final written evaluations to all members of the staff and to set goals for the following year.

A current practice that principals have applauded is getting feedback from the faculty on their own performance. Obviously, this should be done anonymously on a form developed specifically for this purpose. (See Resource 28: Rating Your Middle School Principal.)

Personal Commentary/Notes: _____

_____

* Contact Parents of Students in Danger of Not Graduating

We've mentioned many procedures that should be put in place to avoid surprises for parents whose children are functioning poorly. We strongly recommend sending a letter home to every parent whose child is failing, or may possibly fail, two or more subjects. This can be a form letter signed by the principal and addressed by the secretary.

Personal Commentary/Notes: _____

_____

April Planning

* Establish Summer Vacation and Work Schedules

Develop a calendar of summer work and vacation time for your administrative team, building secretaries, and head custodian. Many principals attempt to have someone in the building all summer to answer questions and to register students. We also request counselors to return two weeks early to schedule new registrants. In this way, all students are scheduled and classes are balanced for the first day of school.

If administrators do not work a 10.5- or 11-month year, make sure to schedule a few days to hold some administrative team meetings.

Personal Commentary/Notes: _____

_____

Finalize Plan for Academic Awards Assembly *

Following a meeting with staff, secure the names of all students who will be receiving departmental or other awards. This allows your secretary or local printers to finalize your moving-up and awards assembly programs. Middle school principals should encourage that service, attendance, and the arts receive equal billing with the academic awards.

Personal Commentary/Notes: _____

_____

Facilitate Planning for Cultural Arts Program *

A culminating program for the cultural arts should be scheduled to demonstrate the work of children in this area. There are times when teachers of art, music, and technology feel that the academic teams get all the attention in modern middle schools. This is their time to shine. Displays with attractive programs should be developed and printed invitations should be sent to all parents. This program provides equal time for the middle school arts program.

Personal Commentary/Notes: _____

_____

April Personnel

*Advertise Teacher Openings **

Although it is the job of the central office to develop a pool of qualified applicants to fill teacher openings, principals can help. Letting your faculty know about any openings in your building and asking them to inform you about candidates they may know can dramatically increase the number of quality candidates. You may also wish to send faculty members to recruitment fairs.

In most buildings, there is a shortage of minority candidates, and in our multicultural society, their recruitment should receive special attention. Some districts are visiting colleges with large minority enrollments to interview graduates. It is a contemporary concern that should be added to our recruiting agenda.

Personal Commentary/Notes: _____

_____

* Celebrate Secretaries' Day

Organizing a celebration for Secretaries' Day will give recognition to some of your most dedicated employees. Every time secretaries do an assignment for teachers, they make your school run more efficiently. When we think of the principal's own secretary, we speak of an efficiency expert, an office manager, and a confidant. When recently addressing a group of retired principals, we were told the former principals miss their secretaries more than anyone else. The honorees of this day truly deserve their accolades.

Personal Commentary/Notes: _____

_____

April Checklists

April Key Tasks

Major Assignments	Date Started	Date Completed	Days on Task
Complete master schedule for coming year			
Conduct new student orientation for fifth graders			
Participate in orientation for eighth graders			
Make public presentation on proposed budget			
Conduct election for student government officers			
Initiate student awards selection process			
Review quarterly report cards			

April Communications

✓	Assignment
	Make PTA presentation
	Attend monthly board of education meeting
	Send congratulatory letter to honor roll students
	Establish parameters for spring musical
	Complete faculty evaluations
	Contact parents of students in danger of not graduating

April Planning

✓	Assignment
	Establish summer vacation and work schedules
	Finalize plan for academic awards assembly
	Facilitate planning for cultural arts program

April Personnel

✓	Finalize
	Advertise teacher openings
	Celebrate Secretaries' Day

April Calendar

MONTH: APRIL

YEAR: ____

MONDAY ____	TUESDAY ____	WEDNESDAY ____	THURSDAY ____	FRIDAY ____	SATURDAY ____
					SUNDAY ____
MONDAY ____	TUESDAY ____	WEDNESDAY ____	THURSDAY ____	FRIDAY ____	SATURDAY ____
					SUNDAY ____
MONDAY ____	TUESDAY ____	WEDNESDAY ____	THURSDAY ____	FRIDAY ____	SATURDAY ____
					SUNDAY ____
MONDAY ____	TUESDAY ____	WEDNESDAY ____	THURSDAY ____	FRIDAY ____	SATURDAY ____
					SUNDAY ____
MONDAY ____	TUESDAY ____	WEDNESDAY ____	THURSDAY ____	FRIDAY ____	SATURDAY ____
					SUNDAY ____

NOTES _____

Chapter
Eleven

He that gives good advice, builds with one hand; he that gives good counsel and example, builds with both.

—Francis Bacon

*I*n most districts, May is the month that school budgets are formally presented to the public for a vote. Outside of large cities, most citizens have the right to vote on these appropriations. If the budget is defeated, there may be an opportunity for a second vote. If not, or if it is defeated for a second time, the district is forced to adopt an austerity budget, which generally forbids the purchase of new equipment and supplies. Austerity budgets can set back the quality of education for several years.

In a recent issue of the National Association of Secondary Schools' *Bulletin* (2002), there was an extremely important article about the Principals' Legislative Action Center (PLAC). It stressed that in the current atmosphere of state budget shortfalls and policy change, it is important to advocate on behalf of your students and school. A quick and easy way to contact your elected officials is to use PLAC, which is available at http://capwiz.com/nassp/home/. This online advocacy tool provides a way to discover not only the contact information of your elected officials but also Action Alerts, which describe current issues and drafts of letters that you can send directly to your elected officials. The U.S. senators and representatives serving on the committees mentioned previously are the most important individuals in the areas of education policy and funding. It's crucial to contact these individuals on matters important to you, your school, and your state. Sharing this information with your PTA leaders and members helps to involve others in this lobbying effort.

We would expect that, if not completed last month, all final classroom evaluations are given the highest priority. Principals should be starting their final evaluations of staff, so the evaluations can be completed before June and principals can set goals with each teacher for the upcoming year. Assuming nontenured-teacher evaluations are completed first and the potential retirees have given notice, hiring of new staff should be in full swing.

Teachers should be a part of the hiring process. Many districts have union contracts that empower their members to be involved. Middle school principals frequently involve teachers because it's consistent with the team philosophy. If a school has only two home and careers teachers, it makes sense for the experienced staff member to be involved in the selection of his or her coworker. Chances are they will even share rooms. We feel this concept is common sense. Staff members on interview committees must complete an in-service course to learn the techniques of the interview process. It is also essential for them to know which questions are illegal to ask. That's why we recommend that interviewers collectively design the questions that will be asked of each candidate.

Conducting a complete review of the present year's budget is now in order. Department chairpersons, teachers, and secretaries should be able to discuss each budget line's excess or shortfall. Ideally, this was done earlier when projecting the following year's budget. The analysis at this time is more accurate and will help with the ordering of supplies and equipment.

Designing the checklist of closing tasks is a massive clerical job. Using last year's file makes the process more manageable and less time-consuming. These forms will be utilized during the closing days in June, so readying them at this time is essential.

Signatures on diplomas, award certificates, and other papers are often legal responsibilities that cannot be delegated. Signing papers now avoids the June rush. Many districts also require the principal's signature on all teacher recommendations, final evaluations, and objectives for the following year. This is why the light is burning late into the evenings in middle school principals' offices. It's not the kind of work one likes to do when school is in session.

One final word about summer school, which is a new, growing responsibility for middle school principals. What was once exclusively a part of the high school principal's job description has become a critical area for development and implementation by middle school principals. One productive idea for the summer is to visit other middle school summer programs. The final design will be your own creation and should meet the specific needs of your school's age group, the school system, and the goals of your staff.

May Key Tasks

MAY

* *Encourage District Budget Vote Participation*

We unashamedly take an active role in getting out our yes votes. In many states, board members and educators are prohibited from using district funds to urge people to vote yes on the school district's fiscal plan. You can, however, encourage everyone to vote. Parents who have children in school are active supporters of the school budget. Principals may legally encourage them to exercise their citizen's right to vote.

Many teacher unions support the schools during the budget vote. They have phone chains to call every teacher who resides in the community to remind them to vote on the school budget. Principals also can ask class mothers to call all parents to do the same. The school budget is one of the few fiscal plans in America where citizens have a right to approve or reject the proposal. Even if we can't tell citizens how to vote, we certainly should encourage their participation in the process.

Personal Commentary/Notes: _____

_____

* *Conduct Monthly Faculty Meeting*

May is a long month for faculty, and often they become tired and frustrated from the demanding school year. Reviewing end-of-year procedures may remind them that we're in the home stretch and that summer vacation is not far away. Any morale booster is practical at this time. One principal invites the PTA to have their teacher recognition day in place of the May faculty meeting. Necessary announcements are communicated via a memo. One reminder must be stressed: Send a final interim report to everyone in danger of failing. When in doubt, send one out.

Personal Commentary/Notes: _____

_____

* *Supervise Interim Report Distribution*

As we noted previously, interim notices generate a multitude of guidance and administrative functions. Letters home from teachers, counselors, and the building principal—as well as teacher-student meetings—are just a few of the essential reactions to the final interim reports. The entire school support staff should be in action mode. In the resource section, you will find an excellent listing of teacher comments for the reports. (See Resource 29: Teacher's Comments for Interim Reports and Report Cards.)

Personal Commentary/Notes: _____

_____

Complete Evaluations of Administrative Team *

The evaluations of your supervisors and administrators should present no surprises for anyone because concerns should have been addressed throughout the school year. Significant issues should have been discussed during frequent on-the-spot meetings or in formal evaluation sessions. There should never be a surprise criticism in any final evaluation. We recommend that the principal request a list of accomplishments from each administrator prior to the evaluation meeting. Hence, principals are reminded of the many services provided by our assistants, which we may have neglected to include in their evaluation. Overlooking certain accomplishments could be potentially damaging to your working relationship. It also makes the supervisory evaluation a two-way process.

Personal Commentary/Notes: _____

_____

Help With Summer School Planning *

By now, the district should have appointed its summer school principal. This is the time to meet with the summer school leader to share your ideas and recommendations. You have finalized, or will shortly be finalizing, your summer work schedule with your head custodian. Knowing this reassures the summer school principal that your plans avoid any possible room conflict for summer school. It's a good idea for the head custodian to join in the meeting for a short period of time, so the two people can meet and briefly discuss what to do if problems arise.

Other issues that should be discussed include the following:

- Curriculum offerings
- Grade reporting procedures
- Information on children with special needs
- Suggestions for staff hiring and class placements
- Textbooks to be used and procedures for the care and return of the books
- Location of curriculum guides for teachers employed from other districts
- Use, and hopefully no abuse, of materials and supplies

- Rooms and equipment not available to the summer school
- Closing procedures and return of keys and materials
- Dropout report and vandalism reports
- Academic results and steps to be taken to disseminate grades to students and counselors

As you can see from the list, although the regular principal does not directly supervise the summer school leader, there is much to discuss.

Personal Commentary/Notes: _____

_____

* Conduct Exit Interviews

Another topic rarely discussed in school improvement plans is the exit interview. Often, the best source of information on the quality of the program and staff comes from the students themselves. Schedule time during this month to meet with your eighth graders in small groups, or even individually, to assess their experiences.

A written survey may be preferred and is simple to design. We suggest you use a teacher committee to develop the document. We never ask students to evaluate individual teachers, since that would be highly unprofessional and would certainly lose teacher support for the evaluation process. We have found that students take the evaluation very seriously if administered in May. If done in June, both humor and negativity are often encountered.

Personal Commentary/Notes: _____

_____

* Conduct Remaining Fire Drills

All required fire and safety drills should be completed this month. The appropriate reporting forms should be completed and sent to the proper authority. There should be no drills during the examination period or during end-of-year activities in June. Nothing should be allowed to upset the building's academic tone.

Personal Commentary/Notes: _____

_____

* Conduct Locker Cleanups

Some principals start this process earlier, but we feel having several in May and early June will suffice. Generally, we allow students to go to their lockers from homeroom to remove excess papers and debris. Our librarians really appreciate this cleanup since many of their overdue books are returned, which helps them process their inventory in a timely fashion. Locker cleanups dramatically reduce the refuse in the building when school ends in June. To allow time for the cleanup, the principal should simply reduce each class by one minute, increase homeroom by ten minutes, and reset the bell schedule.

One of the things you must discuss with your head custodian is the locker cleanup procedure. If it has been organized well, the custodians place large garbage cans in each corridor, and as soon as the children return to their rooms, the floors are swept and the cans removed. No one ever mentions to principals that when they become a principal, they also become a sanitation engineer.

Personal Commentary/Notes: _____

_____

Oversee Administration of Standardized Tests *

This is an increasing responsibility with the advent of numerous state achievement examinations. Since the results are now made public under the Freedom of Information Act, newspapers not only list every score but also compare your percentiles with other buildings and school districts. Unfortunately, these scores have become the most-used data to compare schools. If your school is located in a low socioeconomic community, your results might not represent the quality of your staff's true efforts.

The crisis in middle schools today is that teachers are being forced to abandon the teachable moment and concentrate solely on subject content, drill and practice, and the rigid memorization of facts. The latter is certainly important, but many educators feel that students are losing the spirit of inquiry and the love of learning.

Personal Commentary/Notes: _____

_____

Prepare Report on Goals *

Each year a responsible superintendent or the assistant superintendent should meet with the principal to explore and set goals for the school. These areas might be addressed individually or, more likely, they are created from a team effort. The principal is ultimately responsible for submitting a paper detailing each goal and the activities developed to accomplish the goal. This report is usually incorporated in the principal's evaluation. Usually, a face-to-face meeting is called to review the material and to evaluate the principal's year.

This session produces the principal's personal and building goals for the following year. Most principals report that even though the meeting is always scheduled for May or June, it is often done during the summer. We give our full support to supervision for everyone. If you coast, you can only go downhill. Reasonable expectations generate energy and enthusiasm for administrators and faculty.

Personal Commentary/Notes: _____

_____

May Communications

* *Distribute Progress/ Interim Reports*

Principals should have this at the top of their list for the month of May. We also request that every teacher inform parents about their child's status. If the school has extra classes to help students, parents should know their child has been invited to attend.

Personal Commentary/Notes: _____

_____

* *Complete and Distribute Closing Procedures*

The last days of the school year are always quite busy. They can also be confusing and frustrating if clear procedures are not presented in writing to the staff. Work with your secretaries and the entire supervisory staff to design a sign-out process that avoids long lines and assures the principal that everything needed from teachers is accounted for and, if necessary, returned. Teachers whose rooms will be used for summer school should be informed of this and asked to secure all of their personal material.

Make sure teachers provide you with their summer address or their traveling itinerary. You may have to inform them about an emergency or changes in their assignments. Many principals invite teachers to come in during the summer to serve on interview committees or to work as mentors for new teachers.

This is also the time to culminate plans for a faculty end-of-year party. Having one of your staff members serve as emcee keeps it all in the family. Many faculties recognize colleagues for their extraordinary efforts, while others plan a roast for retirees. The party provides a positive note prior to the rush to leave for vacation.

Personal Commentary/Notes: _____

_____

Give Monthly Presentation at PTA Meeting *

This is the time to recognize parents for their volunteer work and contributions to the school. It's an even better meeting if some appreciative teachers join in the festivities. Principals usually have a supply of pins and T-shirts on hand to present as token gifts to the PTA officers. Some have served the school for three years, and many have been with you even longer if they have a few children. It is, in a sense, their moving-up exercise.

Personal Commentary/Notes: _____

_____

Contact Elementary School Principals *

Your orientation program should be in full swing. Parents of elementary students should be coming to the building for an assembly. Also, middle school counselors should be getting their final recommendations from the fifth-grade teachers. Seek feedback from your elementary colleagues about the orientation program and add these suggestions to your file for next year.

Middle school counselors should now be able to construct the entering sixth-grade classes and teams. We always make sure to have a good balance of students from each elementary school in every class. No student should be isolated from his or her local fifth-grade schoolmates when school begins in September. It's the counselors' responsibility to provide the principal with the names and disabilities of all special needs children and the names of children who should not be grouped together. We recommend that the middle school nurse meet with his or her elementary counterpart to share information about children with serious medical problems. This information should be available to the principal and to every classroom teacher on the first day of classes in September.

Personal Commentary/Notes: _____

_____

May Planning

Begin Developing Activities *
Calendar for the Coming Year

Developing the yearly activities calendar is a complicated task. A special meeting devoted to this job should be held with all extracurricular advisers. The calendar should be coordinated with the high school and the elementary schools because many parents have students at more than one school. Be sure to flag the days before the end of each marking period and highlight all testing dates. A careful check of all religious holidays also helps to avoid conflicts. We should involve our PTA members and other groups who use our buildings after school. If there are adult education classes or neighborhood drama groups in the middle school at night, they too should be asked to submit their dates and their anticipated room use plans.

Personal Commentary/Notes: _____

_____

* Finalize Custodial Summer Work Schedule and Goals

Our goal is to maximize the efforts of our summer custodial and maintenance staff. Specific projects should be listed in priority order. Cleaning of the floors, for example, should be done after the completion of summer school. Remember to host a meeting with the summer school principal, so everyone is aware of which rooms and areas are to be used and which part of the building is closed to students and faculty.

Personal Commentary/Notes: _____

_____

* Analyze Present Year's Budget

In May or early June, we advise principals to review each budget line. Although we did this in preparation for the following year's budget, our findings are now more reliable, and appropriate internal adjustments can be made. Being proactive in this area serves you well throughout the year. If the district allows some emergency purchases at this time, the principal can order some materials that may be nearing depletion. If not, money not used returns to the general fund.

Personal Commentary/Notes: _____

_____

* Plan to Supervise and Attend Spring Events

The principal's school-ending calendar is usually a logistical nightmare. Work with your secretary to block out certain times for class visits and walks through the halls. Be aware of all major night and weekend events you need to attend. Many principals attend every closing activity. If you cannot attend all activities, be sure to avoid appearing as if you favor one sponsored event over another. You will also be invited to many community events and districtwide functions. Try to rotate your participation, and always write notes of regret when your schedule does not permit your attendance.

Personal Commentary/Notes: _____

_____

May Personnel

*Submit Recommendations for * *
Extracurricular Appointments

Most of the extracurricular positions are filled by those who held them the previous year. As the person in charge of staffing, remember to refrain from reappointing faculty members who have not functioned well as advisors. Sometimes filling these positions becomes a challenge. We do recommend giving preference to your own staff members. Unless the teacher contract mandates the hiring from within the district's staff, we try to hire the person who will do the best job for our children. Completing as much of the hiring at this time as possible enables the central office to send out contracts in a timely fashion.

Personal Commentary/Notes: _____

_____

*Complete Extracurricular Activity Report * *

Require each extracurricular advisor to complete and submit an end-of-the-year report. This should include, but is not limited to, a list of meetings held, number and names of participants involved, attendance for each session, and major activities accomplished. A financial accounting should also be made, including the balance in the club's treasury. This information helps the principal decide which clubs and activities to continue to sponsor as well as which advisors to reappoint.

All teachers who serve as advisors should be evaluated and a report of their efforts should be generated. (See Resource 30: Student Activities Evaluation Report.)

Personal Commentary/Notes: _____

_____

* *Conduct Ongoing Teacher Hiring*

Although you are probably overwhelmed with closing responsibilities, hiring new teachers remains a priority. If your staff is to improve, the process starts with the selection of the best available candidates. Although checking references is usually the job of your personnel director, we recommend that principals use their own networking skills to get additional feedback on prospective staff members. Be aware that there are times when a candidate gets a good reference from an unethical administrator who wants to remove the teacher from his or her district. Telephone calls or face-to-face reference inquiries are far superior to written references.

Personal Commentary/Notes: _____

_____

May Checklists

May Key Tasks

Major Assignments	Date Started	Date Completed	Days on Task
Encourage district budget vote participation			
Conduct monthly faculty meeting			
Supervise interim report distribution			
Complete evaluations of administrative team			
Help with summer school planning			
Conduct exit interviews			
Conduct remaining fire drills			
Conduct locker cleanups			
Oversee administration of standardized tests			
Prepare report on goals			

May Communications

✓	Assignment
	Distribute progress/interim reports
	Complete and distribute closing procedures
	Give monthly presentation at PTA meeting
	Contact elementary school principals

May Planning

✓	Assignment
	Begin developing activities calendar for the coming year
	Finalize custodial summer work schedule and goals
	Analyze present year's budget
	Plan to supervise and attend spring events

May Personnel

✓	Finalize
	Submit recommendations for extracurricular appointments
	Complete extracurricular activity report
	Conduct ongoing teacher hiring

May Calendar

MONTH: MAY

MONDAY	TUESDAY	WEDNESDAY	THURSDAY	FRIDAY	SATURDAY
					SUNDAY
					SATURDAY
					SUNDAY
					SATURDAY
					SUNDAY
					SATURDAY
					SUNDAY
					SATURDAY
					SUNDAY

YEAR: ____

NOTES

171

Chapter Twelve

I hear and I forget, I see and I remember, I do and I understand.

—Chinese proverb

For the past few months, we have been planning activities and supervisory tasks that come to fruition in June. If the responsibilities sound familiar, that's because the organization, staffing, and dates were determined earlier this spring. Efficiently closing school is a tribute to the organizational expertise of the middle school principal. We hope this calendar assists principals to attend to a myriad of necessary details that accomplish this end.

The end of a school year is busy, and for most middle school principals, who are both carers and sharers, it also can be quite emotional. An orderly time commitment is impossible to achieve without careful planning and help from the entire staff. Culminating activities of clubs, the PTA, and service organizations often take place outside the school day. Many organizations elect to have these evening events in the community and not in the school. The principal often has more requests for his attendance at events than there are days in the week. Attending as many events as possible is part of a principal's leadership responsibility. There are times, however, when a principal feels comfortable sending another administrator or faculty member to represent the school.

In school, the tone and pace can be even more frenetic. The process of closing activities is compounded by the need for an organized sign-out procedure. The principal's key tasks are numerous and require obsessive attention to detail. A new administrator can easily become overwhelmed because each requirement is important. Any errors or a slowdown in operational efficiency can have a negative ripple effect in summer school and during the following year's opening procedures. Think of the ramifications of the following:

- A retiring teacher not handing in his or her classroom and file cabinet keys
- Incomplete health records for children entering or returning to school in September
- Misplaced final examinations, which are unavailable for parents' review
- Unsigned purchase orders
- Grades not handed in for inclusion on report cards
- Inadequate supervision at one of the final activities

We could go on, but the point is obvious. The teacher sign-out procedures must be completed before teachers receive their final checks. The preparation of the items to be used on this form is the responsibility of the principal, but one requirement must be met: Each item on the sign-out list must be personally initialed by the appropriate supervisor, secretary, or principal. One middle school lists the following items on the final form:

- Class record books
- Attendance registers
- Grade reports
- Failure lists and graded final examinations
- Permanent record cards
- Textbook counts and storage locations
- Report cards for absentees
- Course outlines
- Locker codes and locks
- Keys
- Summer addresses and telephone numbers

Other requirements unique to a principal's building can be added as necessary. The following key tasks validate our contention that middle school principals must be master planners. An annual miracle occurs when all tasks are accomplished in a timely fashion. Many of these duties may be delegated, but the final responsibility is our own.

June Key Tasks

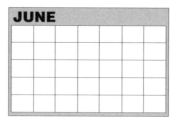

* Monitor Final Examinations

Each year, national surveys reveal that cheating is widespread among all students. Make honesty and security a priority during the administration of final examinations. Meet with examination proctors to review expectations and procedures for handling the supervision of the testing room. Develop a statement to be read by every proctor before the examination begins. Have a supervisor available to handle any questions that come up during the testing period. It also seems practical to select a testing site that discourages cheating.

We have spoken about the security involved in the preparation and storage of the examination papers. When counting papers and distributing them to monitors, the responsibility should be taken seriously. If papers are copied a few weeks before the examination date, they must be stored in a secure area. We prefer a large office safe, if one is available. If not, the subject supervisor should submit a plan for test storage and should get the principal's approval. If we're being overly concerned, think of how you'd feel if a cheating scandal compromised the reputation of your school! Also, sending home the schedule of final examinations keeps everyone informed concerning this important time of year. (See Resource 31: Final Examination Schedule.)

Personal Commentary/Notes: _____

_____

* Issue Final Report Cards

Strict timelines must be adhered to so that all data are entered efficiently. If your report cards are computer generated, a meeting with the technical staff is necessary to develop the schedule of due dates. Procedures informing parents about student failures must be in place if report cards do not go home promptly. As we noted previously, final report card grade submissions are required for teachers to sign out at the end of the school year.

If report cards are mailed, use the opportunity to give parents suggestions on how to help prepare their children for the next grade level. Counselors must remain after the teachers have gone on vacation to answer parents' questions and to register children for summer school.

Personal Commentary/Notes: _____

_____

Review Final Grades *

Subject area supervisors should check every one of their teachers' final grades. Anything unusual should be reported to the principal after a discussion with the teacher. Ultimately, the principal has to make a complete report concerning final examinations and student grades for the superintendent of schools.

The responsible principal should determine grade distribution trends for every teacher and for each department. At times, grading procedures become an evaluation objective for some members of the staff. Also, if students predominantly miss questions on a specific topic, administrators should explore if the subject is adequately covered in the course outline. We can learn a great deal by studying these incorrect responses and assessing poor test results. To be a teacher means we must never stop learning.

Personal Commentary/Notes: _____

_____

Complete All End-of-Year Reports *

With state-required testing, reports are now due to both the superintendent and the designated state officials. Routine items, such as completion of the required number of fire drills, fingerprinting, and assurances that all teachers have state certifications, must be reported. Test results and plans for remediation may be more involved and time-consuming. Double-check each submission because a small mistake may be compounded in any state or district report that is made public.

Personal Commentary/Notes: _____

_____

Organize Final Locker Cleanup *

We detailed the process in our May calendar, but the final job must be completed in June. The cleaning of lockers can also become part of the preparation process for the opening of the next school year. Remember to have each homeroom teacher check every locker after it is cleaned by its assigned student. If there is a need to repair the locker, the teacher should submit the request in writing. The repairs become a custodian's summer assignment. We hope the calendar demonstrates that many chores are interrelated. (See Resource 32: Locker Cleanup.)

Personal Commentary/Notes: _____

_____

* Conduct Moving-Up Exercises

Middle school administrators have moved away from cap and gown graduations. A less formal program serves the needs of this age group and is more in keeping with the middle school philosophy. We want to emphasize that our children have been well prepared for their upward journey to the high school. Middle schools are not an ending to a child's education, and, particularly in lower socioeconomic communities, we want to bring home this point to parents and guardians.

The principal sets the tone for the program at the rehearsal and in communications made to parents of eighth graders. Oversee the distribution of tickets and the production of every aspect of the program. At rehearsals, double-check the spelling and pronunciation of each child's name to avoid embarrassing situations. Specific assignments should be made for supervisors and staff members. At the end of the program, ask for suggestions for improving next year's ceremony.

Personal Commentary/Notes: _____

_____

* Organize and Conduct Awards Assembly

We've already held meetings to determine the criteria and the recipients for every award. The organization of the assembly is the principal's responsibility. It is usually very well attended by parents and community members and serves as an opportunity to demonstrate the best that middle schools have to offer. A well-behaved student body does much to improve the image of the age group and your school.

The pacing of the program should be controlled by the principal. Speakers should be told to make their presentations brief to keep the program moving. Teachers should have reminded their classes about behavioral expectations. Hosting a tea for parents and honored students after the assembly adds a warm final touch.

Personal Commentary/Notes: _____

_____

* Hold Early Registration for Summer School

Students must be given the opportunity to register early for summer school without disrupting the school day. We set aside the afternoon of the last day of classes for this purpose. By then, students know if they have failed classes and can plan their summer accordingly. Registration for enrichment programs can be done during the following week. Again, counselors must be available for this purpose and should flag the student's schedule for any future changes.

Personal Commentary/Notes: _____

_____

Publish Teacher Sign-Out Procedures *

Although we mentioned this in the introduction to this chapter, we have to stress that a comprehensive sign-out procedure must be developed. We've included an example of a sign-out procedure in our resource section for your consideration. (See Resource 33: End-of-Year Sign-Out List.) Set a district-mandated time for the final sign-out, since there is often great controversy over why sign outs were conducted at different times in other buildings. Try to make the process smooth and prompt.

Most principals hold off on other activities at this time to shake hands with every member of the faculty. A brief thank you and personal comment go a long way toward creating a positive ending for your teachers. Make sure that every teacher hands in their sign-out sheet.

Personal Commentary/Notes: _____

_____

Attend Culminating Events *

Try your best to attend as many culminating events as you can, but remember to keep your calendar as clear as possible during the last couple of weeks. June's last-minute details must be attended to. Just as you thanked your faculty during the final sign-out procedures, you must show your appreciation to everyone in the PTA and the community for their help throughout the school year. They were indeed your partners in making the school a success.

Personal Commentary/Notes: _____

_____

Submit Summer Work Recommendations *

Your summer curriculum-writing projects should be in the newly passed school budget. Meet with all staff members involved to provide them with the model on which to base their work. Due dates should be specified. Consideration must be given to their workspace, particularly if you have a large summer school operating in the building. We often use an office or room in an elementary school for this purpose.

Personal Commentary/Notes: _____

_____

* Collect All Outstanding
Books and Equipment

The proper storage of books and equipment is a major undertaking. Work with the staff to create a record-keeping system that is easy to understand and efficient. We strongly recommend that the principal have a key to every room in the building located in a locked cabinet in his or her office. A duplicate set should be kept in a secure location in the head custodian's office. Teachers' keys should be stored in a locked cabinet over the summer. Only the summer school principal should have a key to this cabinet.

A word must be said about the collection of books. Many principals deny students their final report cards until all books are returned. This includes library books and texts. One building supervisor should be responsible for the entire process. Fines and money for lost texts should be collected since they demonstrate our respect for the school's property. Generally, the money collected is returned to the district's general fund. If the money were returned to the individual building's supply code, we believe more strenuous efforts would be made to enforce these collections. Remember to issue receipts to serve as proof that fines were paid and owed materials were returned.

Computers, television sets, and other audiovisual equipment need special care and maintenance. Machines in need of repair should be attended to immediately to make them available for September. A broken machine is not only unusable but also contributes to the diminishing morale of your staff. Since these items are often very expensive, they should be stored in secured areas. To keep them in classrooms with windows facing the exterior of the building is asking for trouble. Getting these items was difficult; now it's up to you to guarantee their security, so they do not have to be replaced after theft.

Personal Commentary/Notes: _____

_____

* Arrange for Fall Sports and Activity Physicals

Most states require all athletes to receive complete physicals prior to the first official tryout practice. Any student who is going to try out for a team must be seen by the school doctor if the student does not have an updated physical from his or her family physician. If formal practices begin in August, the coach is responsible for enforcing this regulation. Children without evidence of a current physical must wait for the nurse to arrange one in September. The proliferation of legal cases makes adherence to this mandate a must.

Personal Commentary/Notes: _____

_____

Transfer Student Records ∗

As soon as counselors have filed all report cards and Individual Educational Programs (IEPs) in the eighth-grade student folders, they should be delivered to the high school. The messenger must receive a signed affidavit from the person who accepts the folders. The middle school principal will also receive the elementary folders for the incoming sixth graders. Since there are sometimes as many as three to six elementary schools within one district, provisions must be made to ensure that all have arrived and have been signed for by a counselor or administrator. If recommending these signatures sounds a bit overcautious, try looking for a missing class of records or an entire elementary school's student folders.

Personal Commentary/Notes: _____

_____

Complete All Required Staff Evaluations ∗

We know most of these were done in May; however, by now, all final evaluations should have been forwarded to the central office's personnel director. Completing all evaluations and filing them in teacher files is important because the teacher file is the only official record of a staff member's performance.

If the principal is really on top of things, the individual teacher goals for the next year will accompany the final evaluations. Knowing these goals when teachers are on summer vacation allows them to take some courses or do some preparation for the forthcoming school year.

Personal Commentary/Notes: _____

_____

June Communications

Write End-of-Year Newsletter ∗

This should be a pleasure to write since it gives you an opportunity to thank the entire staff for their efforts during the past school year. It is also a quick summer correspondence to everyone who worked for you. Any news that will encourage them should be conveyed and is greatly appreciated.

Employing some subtle motivation about the new year is a highly professional technique. Informing the staff members about building improvements and new equipment may also create some enthusiasm. Let them know you are looking forward to seeing them in September. Finally, invite them into the school during the summer if they'd like to visit or go out to lunch with you.

Personal Commentary/Notes: _____

_____

* Promote Faculty Drop-Ins

The invitation to visit mentioned in the previous section is a valuable communication tool for the principal. Meeting with staff over the summer provides a calm atmosphere to discuss potential problems and affords the principal a rare opportunity to gain input from members of the faculty about a myriad of issues. Meetings also improve relationships by making the principal more approachable.

Personal Commentary/Notes: _____

_____

* Make Board of Education Presentation

The June board of education meeting is a time of transition. The newly elected board members are preparing to take office and are anxious to learn about the schools. Use your presentation to highlight the year's accomplishments of staff and students. Identify some goals and special events coming in the next year.

You may also want to invite new board members to tour your building. This is about as political as we get. Our purpose is to make board members aware of our building's needs and to demonstrate areas of pride and faculty resourcefulness. We never take sides in board elections or show preference for one board member over another. Since we have to work with all trustees, we attempt to nurture our relationship with each person.

Personal Commentary/Notes: _____

_____

* Attend PTA Installation Night

This event offers you another opportunity to thank the outgoing officers of your PTA and to welcome those newly elected. If given a place on the agenda, speak about the school's major accomplishments and build enthusiasm for special events planned for the new school year. Let parents know how the middle school is special for their child's age level, and highlight some activities that make the school a home away from home. You may set a date for your summer meeting with the new officers to plan the membership drive and the activities for the next year.

Personal Commentary/Notes: _____

June Planning

Set Deadlines for Submission * *
of Grades and Failure Lists

Failing report card grades and retention are two topics that are of the highest priority this month. Counselors must inform the principal of specific plans developed for each child. This should be done after every option is explained to both the student and his or her parents. If there are no surprises, it means the principal's policies and practices were carried out by every faculty member. It's just one more achievement that only the principal realizes was part of his or her planning expertise.

Personal Commentary/Notes: _____

Finalize Summer Cleaning and Painting Schedule *

Take a few minutes to review your custodians' workload, which was previously jointly developed. If there is an area unable to be completed as planned, the head custodian should share that information immediately. To demonstrate the importance of the summer's workload, the principal should give the head custodian the principal's own summer schedule and phone number. This is an administrative technique that stresses the value a principal places on each job.

Personal Commentary/Notes: _____

Obtain All Teachers' and Chairpersons' *
Schedules and Vacation Dates

We know this was part of the sign-out procedure, but these data must remain close at hand. Knowing summer schedules and vacation dates is critical to gain quick responses to the many questions that arise over the summer. Sudden retirements, concern over a grade, and requests to serve on an interviewing committee are practical examples of the types of issues that need the staff's attention.

Personal Commentary/Notes: _____

_____

* *Develop Preliminary Plans for the Opening of School*

By now, you have begun looking forward to July with your secretarial staff. Welcome-back letters should be drafted. Materials and supplies should begin to be organized. The activity calendar should have approved dates posted. All dates that you wish to appear on the district's calendar should be sent to the central office before you leave for vacation. Take a look at the July calendar and accomplish as many of the required tasks that you can fulfill before closing the books on June.

Personal Commentary/Notes: _____

_____

June Personnel

* *Announce Next Year's Teaching Schedules*

Teachers are always anxious about their schedules for the following year. Coordinate with other administrators and your secretaries to release this information to all staff members at the same time. Be sure to explain that all schedules are tentative because some fine-tuning may be necessary over the summer. We don't recommend the sharing of teacher schedules with parents until the start of school. Scheduling is a principal's responsibility, but asking for teacher preferences for team assignments and grade levels is part of a cooperative management style. The principal has the final decision.

Personal Commentary/Notes: _____

_____

* *Conclude Last-Minute Hiring*

Any teacher or other employee vacancy not filled by the end of June must be included on your summer to-do list. Anyone who is going to work in a school should be interviewed by the principal. This may require you to work on a vacation day. Although others may be involved in the hiring process, we strongly recommend that the principal conclude the process prior to the candidate's final interview with the superintendent. Yes, this goes for aides, secretaries, and custodians as well.

Personal Commentary/Notes: _____

_____

June Checklists

June Key Tasks

Major Assignments	Date Started	Date Completed	Days on Task
Monitor final examinations			
Issue final report cards			
Review final grades			
Complete all end-of-year reports			
Organize final locker cleanup			
Conduct moving-up exercises			
Organize and conduct awards assembly			
Hold early registration for summer school			
Publish teacher sign-out procedures			
Attend culminating events			
Submit summer work recommendations			
Collect all outstanding books and equipment			
Arrange for fall sports and activity physicals			
Transfer student records			
Complete all required staff evaluations			

June Communications

✓	Assignment
	Write end-of-year newsletter
	Promote faculty drop-ins
	Make board of education presentation
	Attend PTA installation night

June Planning

✓	Assignment
	Set deadlines for submission of grades and failure lists
	Finalize summer cleaning and painting schedule
	Obtain all teachers' and chairpersons' schedules and vacation dates
	Develop preliminary plans for the opening of school

June Personnel

✓	Finalize
	Announce next year's teaching schedules
	Conclude last-minute hiring

June Calendar

MONTH: JUNE   **YEAR:** ____

MONDAY ____	TUESDAY ____	WEDNESDAY ____	THURSDAY ____	FRIDAY ____	SATURDAY ____ SUNDAY ____
MONDAY ____	TUESDAY ____	WEDNESDAY ____	THURSDAY ____	FRIDAY ____	SATURDAY ____ SUNDAY ____
MONDAY ____	TUESDAY ____	WEDNESDAY ____	THURSDAY ____	FRIDAY ____	SATURDAY ____ SUNDAY ____
MONDAY ____	TUESDAY ____	WEDNESDAY ____	THURSDAY ____	FRIDAY ____	SATURDAY ____ SUNDAY ____
MONDAY ____	TUESDAY ____	WEDNESDAY ____	THURSDAY ____	FRIDAY ____	SATURDAY ____ SUNDAY ____

NOTES _____

186

Resources

Resource 1
Student Handbook Topics

Academic Misconduct, Cheating, Plagiarism

Academically Gifted Program

Attendance Reporting: Absence, Lateness

Bell Schedule

Bus Passes

Bus Privileges

Bus Transportation

Cafeteria Behavior

Cafeteria Service

Cell Phone Policy

Dances

Detention Policy

Disciplinary Progression

Early Dismissal

Elevator Usage

Extra Help

Field Trip Policy

Fire Drills

Go-Home Evacuation Drill

Guidance Office

Hall Passes

Hat Policy

Health and Medical Services

Homeroom Procedures

Homework Policy

Honor Roll Requirements

Honor Society Membership

Injuries, Proper Reporting Procedures

In-School Suspension

Library Services

Locker Rules and Regulations

Long-Term Absence From School

Lost and Found

Map of School, Room Locations

Medication Regulations

Nurse's Office

Out-of-School Suspension

"Pledge of Allegiance" Regulations

Principal's Office

Progress/Interim Reports

Radio and Headphone Policy

Report Cards

School Closing Procedure

School Dress Policy

School Hours

School Store Service

Smoking Regulations

Spirit Days

Sports Participation Regulations

Stolen Property Reporting Procedures

Student Activities Program

Student Advisors Program

Student Behavior: Rules and Regulations

Student Rights and Responsibilities

Student Signing-In and Out-of-School Policy

Study Tips

Telephone Use Policy

Testing Policy

Textbooks

Use of Internet Policy

Visitors' Policy

Resource 2
Teacher Manual Topics

MEMORANDUM

TO: All the Professional Staff
FROM: Principal
DATE: June
RE: Teacher Manual Revisions

This year's teachers' manual reflected many changes in both format and content. Many hours went into making it more appealing and functional. Its primary purpose remains the same, namely, to serve as a practical guide to our new teachers and to serve as a ready reference to our veterans. Most procedures and practices that we find extant here at our school are included in the manual.

To improve the manual, your input is critical. Along these lines, may I ask for your suggestions for improvement? Please write your suggestions on the attached page and hand them in with your copy of the manual to the main office. Include items for addition or deletion, and feel free to inform us of mistakes of any kind, including spelling, grammar, and, most important, errors in content.

Our intention, as always, is to make our manual a document that is truly reflective of what actually takes place here at our middle school.

The bottom line is if we're going to have a manual, let's make it the best we can.

Topics to Include in Your Middle School Teachers' Manual

Absence: Per Period Attendance

Accident Report Form

Accidents Involving Blood/Bleeding

Accidents or Illness: Standing Orders

Actions to Correct Inappropriate Behavior

Activity Advisors: Guidelines for Conducting an Event

Admission to Class

Library

Long-Term Absence From School: Students

Lost Books

Medical Exemption From Physical Education

Money Collection From Students

Out-of-School Suspension

Parent-Teacher Conference

Participation on Teams/Activities

Passes

Personal Day Requests

Physical Education

Plan Book and Record Book

"Pledge of Allegiance"

Professional Leave Application Forms

Questions and Answers: General

Radios, Cell Phones

Report Cards: Comments List

Reports: Teacher

Seating Charts

Security

Shelter Space

Smoking

Stolen Property Form

Students: Deportment

Students: Leaving Classroom

Students: Leaving School Grounds

Students: Lunch Policy

Students: Rights and Responsibilities

Students: Signing In or Out of School

Substitute Enrichment Program

Substitute-Teacher Instruction

Supplies: Requisition Form

Suspensions

Teacher Absence

Teacher Absence Report Form

Television

Textbook Adoption Form

Textbooks

Truancy

Unreturned Books

Use of Building by Outside Groups

Use of Building Form

Use of Building on Weekends and Holidays

Work Request Form

Resource 3
How to Build a Mission Statement for School Improvement

Many schools are like rudderless ships, riding the waves of fad and reform from one end of the education spectrum to the other. Innovation and change in schools frequently mirror innovation and change in society as a whole; however, due to the diversity of public opinion and expectations regarding the role of the schools, individuals and groups in society may not agree about the role of schools, regardless of the current trends and fads.

These disagreements may be based on cognitive versus affective, individual versus societal, vocational versus academic, and religious versus secular ideas.

As these different emphases pull against one another, the rudder of the school turns from side to side in a futile effort to accommodate all.

When faced with this situation, an effective school demonstrates the characteristics of a high-performance organization with a common mission as a foundation, able to steer its own course through the maze of societal hopes and expectations.

Effective schools confront conflicting societal expectations with a firm sense of where they are headed. While not discounting the wishes of parents and other community groups, they clearly state their priorities from the outset.

A written mission statement is a highly visible feature of effective schools. In addition to stating the school's priorities, it reflects the commitment of the administration and staff to the school's mission.

The Role of the Principal

Staff members will probably not feel a common sense of mission unless the principal has taken an active role in formulating and articulating that mission. This role may include direct involvement in the formulation of the statement, the writing of the statement, or at least close contact with the committee charged with writing the statement.

Leaders of effective schools operate with a dual vision of where they see the school now and what they see it becoming in the future. Whatever their leadership style, they concentrate on those activities that close the gap between the two.

The mission statement is an important vehicle whereby the principal may communicate this dual vision to staff, students, and the community and give purpose to the daily activities of the school. Too often, principals see their role as one of managing what is rather than leading toward what could be. Such administrators may relate well to staff members and students and may effectively maintain the daily routine, but they are not leaders whose actions motivate staff and students toward significant school improvement.

Administrators must not be afraid to express their conceptions of a good school and its mission for fear they will stir up trouble. They can provide valuable, useful guidance. Above all, leaders of high-performing systems carry out the mission of their organization.

Developing a Mission Statement

Developing a mission statement and articulating a sense of mission requires effort, perseverance, communication, human relations skills, a sense of vision, and a willingness to publicly affirm one's beliefs. When developing a mission statement, principals should consider the following:

- The mission statement must be clearly articulated. Some administrators communicate a sense of mission by example (e.g., symbolic actions, time allocations), others by persuasion.

- The committee charged with writing the mission statement should include volunteers representing all of the different subgroups within the staff and community; race, sex, and age equity are vital.

- Academic, vocational, and special education teachers should be represented, as well as parents and retired persons from the community.

- In spite of the heterogeneous makeup of the group, the committee members should share a commitment to base the mission statement on group consensus; the statement should reflect the beliefs on which everyone agrees.

- As a starting place, the committee might solicit staff and community members' views about their philosophy of education, child growth and development, and the roles of teachers and parents in this process. A brief questionnaire might accomplish this first step.

- Once committee members begin drafting the mission statement, frequent communication among committee members, staff members, and community members is important.

- Representatives from these groups should have the opportunity to review and edit successive drafts of the statement. The principal should play an important role as a communications liaison.

- The document should be written in short, logically connected statements that clearly reflect specific goals. During the revision process, superfluous statements will be eliminated, so the final drafted form does not exceed one page.

- When completed, the mission statement should be posted throughout the school: in the main office, the hallways, and in each classroom.

- Copies can also be displayed in local community centers and businesses and anywhere people connected with the school gather. A copy should also be sent to every parent.

- The mission statement should serve as a guide in orientation sessions for new staff members, students, parents, and school visitors. Principals should rely on the statement to explain the rationale for any school policy or practice.

- The administration and staff should consciously strive, through word and action, to symbolize their commitment to the mission statement.

- At some point, students, especially those at the secondary level, should be encouraged to develop their own mission statement. Many of the suggestions listed here would apply to a student mission statement.

- Program, policy, and procedural changes within the school should take place with the mission statement in mind. It should serve as the rationale for change.

- Do not allow the mission statement to become a philosophical straitjacket; avoid carving the statement in stone. The committee members should periodically review the statement for possible revisions.

- High-performing, instructionally effective schools are characterized by a consensus regarding the school's basic goals.

That such schools are able to remain on course while besieged by the demands and expectations of society is due, in part, to the fact that they know where they are headed.

Resource 4
How Parents Can
Help Their Children Succeed

Dear Parents/Guardians,

Oftentimes prior to the beginning of a new school year, parents ask for advice in helping their children get off to a good start in school. Surveys show that an overwhelming number of students feel their teachers do a great job teaching and that schools do a good job teaching subject matter. However, we all know that schools can't do it all. Parents can play a vital role in helping youngsters develop strong study skills.

The following ideas come from several articles, and I believe they will provide some useful suggestions:

- Help children use a planning calendar and notebook to keep track of weekly, monthly, or large projects.

- Encourage children to break down large complex tasks into manageable pieces.

- Complete homework tasks in some order of priority. (Sometimes, it's best to do the least-favorite task first.)

- Don't be too concerned if your child's notes look sloppy or a bit disorganized. Active minds organize things in ways that work best for them. We've learned this from research on learning styles.

- Encourage young readers to use all the clues available to them while reading headlines, pictures, captions, charts, tables, and graphs.

- A discussion with children after reading a book or article helps with comprehension. Ask your child to tell you what the story was about, why or why not it interested them, and perhaps how it might relate to their own lives.

Should you need more in-depth information, you can always talk to your child's teacher. He or she can provide a clearer picture of your child's learning style, strengths, and weaknesses. Also, remember, if I may be of help in this or any other matter, please feel free to call me.

With best personal regards,

Your Middle School Principal

Resource 5
Building Inspection Checklist

First Floor

_____ *Exterior doors.* Are they locked?
_____ *Courtyard.* Does it need weeding?
_____ *Lobby.* Are benches secure and sturdy?
_____ *Auditorium doors.* Are they working properly?
_____ *Cafeteria.* Check general appearance.
_____ *Garbage pails.* Are hall, classroom, and office garbage pails empty?
_____ *Windows.* Is there any broken glass?
_____ *Display cases.* Is the condition of showcases satisfactory?
_____ *Phone booths.* Are they clean and free of graffiti?

Second Floor

_____ *Ceiling lights.* Are they all working?
_____ *Windows.* Are there any broken windows?
_____ *Floors.* Are all floors clean and dust free?
_____ *Walls and stairwells.* Is there graffiti that needs to be removed?
_____ *Bulletin boards.* Is there any damage?
_____ *Stairwell handrails.* Are they secure?
_____ *Fire door/fire exit windows.* Are these emergency exits accessible and in working order?
_____ *Exit lights.* Are they working properly?
_____ *Fire alarm boxes.* Are they secure? Do they need batteries?
_____ *Fire extinguishers.* Are they where they should be? Are their inspections up-to-date?
_____ *Hallway garbage cans.* Are they empty?
_____ *Water fountains.* Are they working properly?
_____ *Lockers.* Are any frames loose? Do any need paint? Do any have graffiti to be removed or painted over? Do doors need repair?
_____ *Ceiling tiles.* Are any in need of repair?
_____ *Rooms.* Are garbage pails empty? Are any windows broken? Are any blinds in need of repair?
_____ *Bathrooms.* Check for leaks. Check for graffiti. Are all lights working? Is toilet paper available?
_____ *Bathroom sinks.* Are faucets and drains working properly? Are hand dryers working properly?

Exterior Check

_____ *Flag.* Is it raised? Is it in need of repair?

_____ *Grounds.* Is there garbage on the premises?

_____ *Parking lot.* Is there broken glass? Do parking lines or numbers need repainting?

_____ *Tennis courts.* Is general appearance acceptable? Are tennis nets set up?

_____ *Windows.* Are any windows broken?

_____ *Building fascia.* Is any of the aluminum fascia loose or missing?

_____ *Trees.* Are any branches too low and or in need of trimming? Do any shrubs need trimming?

_____ *Paint.* Do any doors or any trim need painting?

_____ *Security lights.* Are light covers broken? Are they working properly?

_____ *Fences.* Are any fences in need of repair?

_____ *Cobblestones.* Are any loose?

_____ *Signs.* Are any signs defaced or missing?

_____ *Gas main.* Is protective fencing in good shape?

Resource 6
Sample Interim/Progress Report

To the Parents/Guardians of:

_____

Student Name:

_____

Student's Address:

_____

_____

Interim / Progress Report Quarter 2—November 12 to December 14

Student Name: _____

Grade Level: 8

Student ID #: _____

Counselor's Name: _____

Term	Period	Course Title	Teacher	Comments
Full Year	1	Science	A	Doing well in class discussions Homework accurate and on time
Full Year	HR	Attendance	B	
Full Year	2	Math	C	Excellent test grades
Full Year	3	Social Studies	D	Respectful Contributes to class discussions
FY-Alt Days	4A	Technology	E	Work is improving
FY-Alt Days	4B	Band	F	Outstanding effort
Full Year	5	Physical Ed.	G	Excellent participation
Full Year	6	Lunch	H	
S1-Half Year	7	Art	I	Very cooperative
S2-Half Year	7	Health	J	
Full Year	8	English	K	Writing skills need improvement

The following is a report of cumulative absences and tardies for the school year to date:

Absences: 7

Tardies: 2

If you have any questions or concerns, please contact the guidance office.

Some Dates of Interest:

1/5   Site-based meeting at 5 P.M. in room 126
1/7   Parent-teacher conference night (A–L) 7:00 P.M.–9:00 P.M.
1/9   Middle school New Year's dance 7:00 P.M.–9:30 P.M.
1/14   Parent-teacher conference night (M–Z) 7:00 P.M.–9:00 P.M.

Resource 7
Middle School
Substitutes' Memorandum

Date: _____

Substitute for: _____

Room: _____

Your assignments for today are as follows:

		Regular Teacher	Subject
7:35 A.M.–8:17 A.M.	Period 1		
8:20 A.M.–9:08 A.M. (includes six-minute homeroom)	Period 2		
9:12 A.M.–9:54 A.M.	Period 3		
9:58 A.M.–10:40 A.M.	Period 4		
10:44 A.M.–11:26A.M.	Period 5		
11:30 A.M.–12:12 P.M.	Period 6		
12:16 P.M.–12:58 P.M.	Period 7		
1:02 P.M.–1:44 P.M.	Period 8		
1:48 P.M.–2:30 P.M.	Period 9		

Guidelines for Substitutes

1. Review assignment with secretary.

2. Locate teacher's plan book, seating chart, and air raid and fire drill instructions.

3. Make sure you meet classes in assigned rooms promptly to avoid discipline problems.

4. No student may leave the room without a pass. Only one student may sign out at a time.

5. If a child wishes to make a phone call, he or she must get permission from the main office.

6. As the previous items indicate, homeroom has become a part of the second period class. Please take attendance and list the names of those students absent. Send the list to the office at the end of the

homeroom period (via one student). Please include any absent notes that may be handed in. Sixth graders' attendance is taken during first period and sent to the office immediately.

7. Report any difficulties to the main office immediately. In addition, list the names of any unruly students on the reverse side of this sheet.

8. Return this sheet to the main office at the end of the school day, together with the completed unexplained absence form (names of students who are not listed as absent but who do not appear in your class, that is, are cutting). It is important for us that you list specific names of students and not say the class was a "good" or "bad" class. If you are specific, we can follow through with appropriate disciplinary action.

For Substitute Teachers: Procedures Regarding Discipline

All students are expected to behave well when a substitute teacher is present. If there are any problems with a student, the substitute may use the following techniques:

1. Inform the student that misbehavior in class will result in a letter sent home to his or her parents/guardians from the principal. To ensure that this happens, please list the student's name on the substitute teacher report.

2. If the student is disrupting the class, you may send the child to the detention room following these procedures:
   a. All such students must be escorted by another student.
   b. The escorting student should take the disciplinary referral slip and a pass to the detention room. (Please take the time to write out the Detention Room Referral slip). If the student was so disruptive as to be referred to the principal, the point is underlined to the whole class by your taking the time to write out the referral.
   c. If, in your judgment, the offending incident requires the immediate attention of the principal, please indicate this sense of urgency on the referral.
   d. For help in your classroom, send a message to the main office, and your request will get immediate attention.
   e. When you send a student to the detention room, be sure to fill out a discipline referral and leave it in the office at the end of the day.

THE DETENTION ROOM IS LOCATED IN ROOM 209

Substitute Teacher Report

1. Were plans available: _____

2. Reaction to day:

_____

_____

_____

_____

_____

3. Homeroom teachers please list names of absentees:

_____   _____

_____   _____

_____   _____

_____   _____

_____   _____

_____   _____

4. Any message to the regular teacher:

_____

_____

_____

_____

_____

5. Student behavior problems: (List names and provide a brief comment about the problem.)

_____

_____

_____

_____

_____

6. Suggestions:

_____

_____

_____

_____

_____

Substituted for: _____

Date: _____

Name of substitute: _____

Regular Teacher Return From Absence Report

1. Did substitute teacher follow your plans?

_____

_____

2. Was there any unusual student reaction?

_____

_____

3. Would you like this teacher to substitute for you again?

_____

_____

4. Suggestions:

_____

_____

Teacher's name: _____

Date: _____

Name of substitute: _____

Resource 8
Characteristics of
the Middle School Child

*L*ife itself is an exaggeration during the period of time that children leave the security of their local elementary school until they survive the first year of high school. Grades six through nine, no matter what name we give to the institution, force students to confront life when they are most uncomfortable with their own bodies and minds. The physical awkwardness accompanying the onset of puberty, the unquenchable desire for peer acceptance, and the need to test the author of parents, adults, and society's taboos, create an inner turmoil which makes each day a struggle for survival. These factors make teaching at the middle school level so much more than imparting data. The learner will rarely be a passive listener and the instructor must constantly be aware of the inner turmoil being experienced by each member of the class.

In the contemporary middle school, the sixth grade students bears little resemblance to those in the eighth grade. Sixth grade teachers can expect a child who:

- Is comfortable with adults
- Likes teachers and school
- Does not challenge the authority of teachers or parents
- Is relatively satisfied with his or her appearance
- Enjoys other children
- Is excited and somewhat fearful about moving up to the middle school

Changes begin for most children in the seventh grade and are usually pronounced in the eighth grade. Many years ago these differences were attributed more to boys than to their female classmates. Today, young women seem to be maturing earlier and thus present a similar challenge to teachers and parents. As one observes an eighth grade class, girls often look older and can be more physically mature than their male classmates. It is not unusual to see girls taller than boys at eighth grade dances.

During the seventh and eighth grade there is a radical change in middle school students. Obviously, some physically mature earlier than others. However, attitudes and behaviors seem to become much more challenging toward teachers, parents, and adults. The child in the eight grade assumes a host of more difficult characteristics than his sixth grade counterpart. Eight graders are likely to be:

- Uncertain about other people, especially adults
- More open to peer relationships than to family or adults
- Less communicative and even a bit withdrawn
- Increasingly difficult in classroom situation because their need to impress peers seems to be more important than their desire to satisfy teachers

- Suspicious of adults
- Uncomfortable with their bodies and intensely worried about peer acceptance
- Enjoying the intellectual challenge of a variety of teachers, classes, and extracurricular activities
- Fiercely loyal to peers
- Quite different in their relationships with parents and siblings; this change is generally not clam and passive and often necessitates a major readjustment in the family's interpersonal relationships
- More challenging to all authority figures in school, the home, and society

The recognition of these characteristics of middle school children presents a significant challenge to their teachers. These are factors middle school staff members should consider when planning lessons and activities. Reviewing these changes in behavior of young people should be a part of the principal's inservice program for new staff members. Additionally, they are worthy of periodic review by the entire staff.

Resource 9
Building Security Memo

MEMORANDUM

TO: All Staff
FROM: Principal
DATE: October
RE: Building Security

The security of our school building is always a concern.

In an effort to consolidate our forces, we ask that you take the following actions:

1. When you leave your room at the end of the day, please make sure your windows are closed and locked. This is a must for teachers who have classrooms located on the first floor.

2. It's a good idea to lock your room whenever you leave for any length of time, and this is a must at the end of the day.

3. Teachers should place their grade books in a secure place. The same advice applies to pocketbooks, keys, wallets, and so on. A locked file cabinet goes a long way in preventing unwanted losses.

4. As you walk about the building, take note of anything suspicious that might lead to a problem. Usually, we can nip a potential problem in the bud if we get an early tip from you. Writings on a wall or marks on a door may be the early warning signs of a student in need of help. Please notify one of the administrators when something seems amiss. Don't wait until it's too late.

5. Students should not be allowed out of your class without a pass. Please limit the number of passes that you issue.

6. When you notice someone who looks like they're up to no good, notify the office immediately. Be sure to take note of the time, the location, and as many details as soon as you can. Such details seem insignificant but often prove to be the missing pieces to a larger picture.

In conclusion, our school is a safe school. By far the vast majority of our students are decent and honest. They respect us as educators and appreciate our efforts to make them better people. The number of disruptive students is minimal in comparison, but since one rotten apple can spoil the bunch, we must be ever vigilant to combat their activities. The suggestions outlined here should help keep our school free of unnecessary acts of vandalism and preserve our well-earned reputation as a great place to be.

As always, thanks for your cooperation.

Resource 10
Principal's Orientation
Presentation

To Teachers New to the School District Orientation Agenda

Student Activities and Coaching

- Discuss the types of clubs and organizations offered at our middle school
- Distribute copies of the Student Activities Guidebook
- Discuss the hiring of advisors process
- Remind them that their attendance at student events is noticed, especially by students

Our Student Activities Participation Policy

- Discuss its overall purpose
- Discuss how it works
- Explain the teacher's role and the advisor's role

Audience Control

- Discuss the overall purpose of having teachers serve as audience control monitors
- Explain how teachers are chosen to work as audience control monitors
- Discuss what is appropriate supervision (distant nearness, common sense, etc.)
- Remind them to exhibit professional conduct at events, such as dances

Grading Policies at Our Middle School

- Grade books: How often should you test?
- What criteria will make up a student's grade? Remind them to inform the students of their policy in writing.
- When are grades due?
- When are interims due? Who should receive an interim (bad and good)?
- What are scan forms?
- What are verification sheets?
- How can teachers correct mistakes?

Miscellaneous Concerns

- Suggest that they use the buddy system their first year
- Remind them to read the Teachers' Manual
- Discuss discipline progression
- Stress the importance of seating charts
- Remind them to tell their classes what is expected and to be prepared to enforce their policies
- Discuss issuing passes (in school: okay under certain circumstances; out of school, not okay)
- Discuss after-school availability
- Discuss per-period attendance
- Remind them that visitors to their classes are not permitted
- Remind them to lock doors and cabinets when they are not around
- Discuss the importance of fire drills (eight in the fall, four in the spring); remind them to bring grade books, to lock doors
- Remind them to keep valuables—grade books, keys, field trip money, wallets, pocketbooks—out of sight
- Discuss paycheck dates and procedures
- Discuss lesson plan books (use a notebook)
- Discuss teacher absences
- Discuss accident reports (better safe then sorry)
- Discuss the use of the emergency call box keys
- Suggest that they take a first-aid course and get certified
- Remind them that all visitors to the building should have passes from the main office
- Discuss emergency windows and to keep them accessible
- Discuss rules for eating in the classroom; remind them that some students do not have a scheduled lunch period
- Discuss issuing passes to the nurse's office, to the telephone, and so forth
- Remind them to close all windows at the end of the day, especially the last teacher who uses a room
- Remind them to turn all lights out if the room will be unused the following period and at the end of the day
- Discuss the Initiate Custodial Work request form

Handouts

- First-Quarter Grade Reporting memo
- Copy of a scan form
- Student Activities Guidebook
- Audience control assignment sheet for coverage of a middle school event

Resource 11
Principal's Weekly Bulletin

Principal's Weekly Bulletin—Friday, October

1. As we enter the fifth week of school, allow me to extend a sincere thank you for a great start of another school year. Obviously, your efforts made this possible!

2. Thanks for your participation in last week's Open School Night. Many parents have sent complimentary letters noting the informative and friendly nature of this annual event. Evenings such as this one help our parents to see and understand what a fine and dedicated faculty you are.

3. The middle school PTA provides us with a large amount of support for all we do. All of their fundraising efforts help support our programs and our kids. Remember, the *T* in PTA is an important element in this organization since it symbolizes the joining together of many constituencies of the school community. Soon, the PTA Membership Committee will be putting a reminder in your mailboxes asking you to become an active member. Let's get the number of faculty members in the 90 to 100% range! Thank you for joining.

4. We are coming up to the end of the first interim period. We request that you use the available comments broadly and provide feedback to as many parents and students as possible. Many of our parents appreciate knowing how their youngsters are doing, so try to give each student a comment or two.

5. The field trip season is upon us. Please remember to place the date of an upcoming trip on the Field Trip Calendar (located in the attendance office) to help us monitor the number of trips going out on any one day. Also, please don't forget the ten-day requirement for submitting the list of students going on the trip. These rules help make things go so much smoother.

Next Week's Activities of Note

Monday Oct 5 (a 5 day)	Field trip to Museum of Modern Art (9:00 A.M.–2:00 P.M.) All art classes Supervisory cabinet meeting
Tuesday Oct 6 (a 6 day)	Teacher training course: Introduction to Word Processing, room 357 Parents' sports club meeting 7:30 P.M.

Wednesday	Cognitive abilities testing of new entrants
Oct 7 (a 1 day)	New teacher orientation meeting with the principal in room 112
Thursday	Eighth-grade class picture: Period 2 in the gym
Oct 8 (a 2 day)	Board of education meeting 8:00 P.M.
Friday	Field trip to the county court house 9:00 A.M.
Oct 9 (a 3 day)	First-quarter interims are due on Monday

Resource 12
Effective Teamwork
and Group Leadership

The group . . .

1. Has a clear understanding of its purpose or goals.

2. Makes progress toward its goals with maximum efficiency.

3. Is able to look ahead and plan ahead.

4. Has achieved a high degree of intercommunication.

5. Is able to initiate and carry on effective problem solving.

6. Is objective about its own functioning, can face its own problems and make whatever modifications are needed, and maintains a balance between emotional and rational behavior.

7. Strikes an appropriate balance between group productivity and the satisfaction of individual needs.

8. Provides for sharing of leadership responsibilities by group members.

9. Provides an atmosphere in which members freely express their feelings and points of view.

10. Achieves an appropriate balance between the regular agenda and the hidden agenda (i.e., difficulties in personal relationships that must be worked out before members are free to cooperate effectively with one another).

11. Has a high degree of cohesiveness or solidarity but not to the point of stifling individuality.

12. Makes intelligent use of the differing abilities of its members.

13. Faces reality and sticks to issues that are vital to its members.

14. Is not dominated by its leader or by any of its members.

15. Recognizes that means are inseparable from ends.

16. Recognizes the values and limitations of democratic methods.

SOURCE: Adapted from Haiman (1951).

Resource 13
Best Practices in Quality Education for Students With Severe Disabilities

Inclusion. Students with disabilities are welcomed into their communities, schools, and regular education classrooms. Students attend their home schools (the schools they would attend if they did not have a disability) and access the total school environment.

Functional curriculum. Students are taught clusters of skills and activities that have direct practical applications within their daily lives. Age-appropriateness: Materials, activities, and interactions are appropriate to students' chronological ages (not so-called mental ages).

Individually adapted curriculum and instruction. Curriculum, instruction, and support strategies are designed to meet the individual needs of each student. All necessary modifications to meet students' programmatic or support needs are provided within inclusive school and community environments.

Community-referenced instruction. As students get older, they are provided instruction in recreation and leisure, domestic/home living, general community functioning, and vocational environments within the school and community.

Home-school collaboration. School and family practice a team approach to the educational process. Parents are involved as active and visible participants in decision making throughout the school years.

Circles of friendship and support. Students experience the support network of peers. They need to be included within their classrooms, schools, and communities. When necessary, teams of adults and children work together to problem solve how students with disabilities can be fully included.

Integrated therapy for related services. Related services (e.g., speech/language, physical therapy, occupational therapy) support students' participation in school and community environments. Educational and therapeutic techniques are cooperatively designed to assess, plan, implement, evaluate, and report progress on educational needs and goals. Therapists provide both direct service to students and indirect consultative services to other educators.

Positive approaches to challenging behavior. Nonaversive interventions are used to address behavior problems. The purposes or functions of a problem behavior are identified, and team members problem solve and design strategies for preventing the behavior, teaching alternative desirable skills to meet this function or purpose, and reacting appropriately if the behavior does occur.

Resource 14
Open School Night
Memo to Teachers

MEMORANDUM

TO: All Teachers
FROM: Principal
RE: Open School Night: September 26

I would like to offer some pertinent reminders relative to our upcoming presentations during the evening of September 26. Please remember that the class periods are limited to ten (10) minutes. Therefore, please start on time and make effective use of the time available.

1. Be positive about your class. Indicate educational and intellectual importance and college and career value. Be upbeat about your district, school, and class.

2. Separate academics from discipline and punishment procedures.

3. Review your expectations, requirements, and homework procedures as related to the curriculum of your course. Please distribute some type of handout. In general, parents feel positive when they take away some document that explains requirements. It is also desirable not to read from the handout during your presentation.

4. Please explain your schedule and location for extra help. Remember that your extra help schedule is to be posted in your classroom(s).

5. Open School Night is not a time for personal conferences. I suggest that you do not bring your grade books.

6. To avoid uncomfortable moments, it is of value to review the Health List and Special Education Student List prior to the evening.

7. Experience-based comments: Please do not criticize other schools, grade levels, teachers, departments, central office, and so on. Such comments detract from all of our efforts.

8. Reassure parents that you will communicate both positive and negative concerns.

Please remember that on Open School Night, you represent the school, the district, the board, and the profession. Your dress, demeanor, and statements should convey a professional and exemplary approach to your job. Remember to come early for the best parking.

We will be following an A Day schedule.

Resource 15
Budget Process Calendar

The budget calendar lists the activity to be performed, the responsible party, and the approximate time frame and will begin with the person in the central office responsible for preparing the information and process.

Activity to Be Performed	Responsibility	Time Frame
1. Prepare budget preparation information	Asst. Supt./Bus.	By 11/19
2. Prepare enrollment projections	Asst. Supt./Pers.	By 12/3
3. Prepare building-level administrative and instructional expense requests for supplies, materials, and equipment	Principals and building-level staff	By 12/17
4. Prepare building-level personnel requests for expense, classified and nonclassified	Principals and building-level staff	By 1/7
5. Prepare building-level expense requests, plant operation and maintenance and custodial supplies and materials	Supt. Buildings and Grounds, principals, and custodians	By 1/7
6. Prepare building-level expense requests for custodial personnel	Supt. Buildings and Grounds, principals, and head custodians	By 1/7
7. Prepare expense estimates, fuel, utilities, etc.	Supt. Buildings and Grounds	By 1/14
8. Review plant operation and maintenance expense requests	Supt. and Asst. Supt./Bus.	By 1/19
9. Review of various levels of negotiations, budgetary impasse	Chief Negotiator, Supt. and Asst. Supt./Bus.	By 1/19
10. Prepare expense requests: special education, psychiatric services, handicapped, per diem, homebound and extracurricular	Asst. Supt./Pers.	By 1/19
11. Prepare regular transportation expense requests	Asst. Supt./Bus.	By 1/21
12. Prepare special transportation expense requests	Asst. Supt./Bus./Pers.	By 1/21
13. Prepare expense requests, gas, oil, supplies, materials, repairs, etc.	Asst. Supt./Bus.	By 1/21
14. Prepare capital improvements requests	Supt. and Asst. Supt./Bus.	By 1/28
15. Prepare undistributed expense requests, retirement, social security, health insurance	Asst. Supt./Bus.	By 1/28
16. Review and revise (if necessary) service, expense requests	Asst. Supt./Bus.	By 1/28

(Continued)

Activity to Be Performed	Responsibility	Time Frame
17. Revise enrollment projections	Asst. Supt./Pers.	By 1/28
18. Review transportation expense requests	Asst. Supt./Bus.	By 2/4
19. Review and finalize summary school budget	Asst. Supt./Bus.	By 2/4
20. Prepare BOCES budget expense requests	Asst. Supt./Bus.	By 2/4
21. Review material and supplies budget requests with principals	Central office	Week of 2/7
22. Review equipment budget requests with principals	Central office	Week of 2/7
23. Review materials and supplies with directors	Central office	Week of 2/7
24. Review equipment with directors	Central office	Week of 2/7
25. Compile initial budget request and compare with initial program objectives	Asst. Supt./Bus.	Week of 2/22
26. Review and revise budget requests	Asst. Supt./Bus.	Week of 2/22
27. First complete review by Budget Advisory Comm.		Week of 2/22
28. Finalize staffing		Week of 2/22
29. Finalize enrollment projection	Asst. Supt./Pers.	Week of 2/22
30. Budget Advisory Committee recommendations considered and reviewed		Week of 3/1
31. Final compilation of budget	Asst. Supt./Bus.	Week of 3/1
32. Budget presented to board of education		Week of 3/7
33. Board of education meeting with Budget Advisory Committee		Week of 3/14
34. Board of education adopts budget		Week of 4/11
35. Budget brochure completed and released		Week of 4/25
36. School district annual meeting and vote	Asst. Supt./Bus.	Week of 5/20

Resource 16
Interim Progress Reports Memo

MEMORANDUM

TO: All Faculty
FROM: Principal
DATE: September 30
RE: Interim Progress Reports: Friday, October 4

This is a reminder about the philosophy that guides our approach to sending interim reports to families. All students should receive an interim progress report.

There is great value in formally communicating to families at the midpoint prior to the November report card mailings. Progress reports provide us with the opportunity to give families a snapshot of student performance and a preview of how their child is performing to date. Comments that address concerns and areas of strength are greatly appreciated. Please use this communication mechanism to share positive comments as well as areas for improvement!

With this in mind, please follow the procedures and timelines for submitting your student comments for this first interim reporting period. Since we have migrated to a new student management system, we will have to manage the process differently until we are fully operational.

Accompanying this memo please find a list of possible student comments and a class roster for each section that you teach. Using the class roster with the comment grid, list the code number that corresponds to the comment you are making about this student, and enter up to three comments per student. If a student is in your class but is not listed on the roster, print his or her name at the bottom of the page along with the comments.

After you have completed an interim progress report for each child in your class, please submit the class rosters to the main office on or before Tuesday, October 1, at 8:00 A.M. We will then enter the information into the new system and print the reports for distribution. Your anticipated cooperation is greatly appreciated.

Resource 17
Attention-Deficit Disorders

Suggested Classroom Accommodations for Specific Behaviors

Although the information provided here is designed for use with students with attention-deficit disorders, much of it is useful for students with a wide range of learning disabilities.

When You See This Behavior	*Try This Accommodation*
1. Difficulty following a plan with high aspirations but lacks follow-through; sets out to get straight As, ends up with Fs (sets unrealistic goals)	Assist student in setting long-range goals; break the goal into realistic parts. Use a questioning strategy with the student. Ask, "What do you need to be able to do this?" Keep asking that question until the student has reached an obtainable goal. Have student set clear timelines for what he or she needs to do to accomplish each step. (Monitor student's progress frequently.)
2. Difficulty sequencing and completing steps to accomplish specific tasks (e.g., writing a book report, term paper, organizing paragraphs, division problems)	Break the task into workable and obtainable steps. Provide examples and specific steps to accomplish the task.
*3. Shifting from one uncompleted activity to another without closure	Define the requirements of a completed activity. For example, "Your math is finished when all six problems are complete and correct; do not begin on the next task until it is finished."
*4. Difficulty following through on instructions from others	Gain student's attention before giving directions. Use alerting cues. Accompany oral directions with written directions. Give one direction at a time. Quietly repeat directions to the student after they have been given to the rest of the class. Check for understanding by having the student repeat the directions. Place general methods of operation and expectations on charts displayed around the room and on sheets to be included in student's notebook.
5. Difficulty prioritizing from the most to least important	Prioritize assignments and activities. Provide a model to help the student. Post the model and refer to it often.
6. Difficulty sustaining effort and accuracy over time	Reduce assignment length and strive for quality rather than quantity. Increase the frequency of positive reinforcements. Catch the student doing it right and let him or her know it.
7. Difficulty completing assignments	List or post (and say) all steps necessary to complete each assignment. Reduce the assignment to manageable sections with specific due dates. Make frequent checks for assignment completion. Arrange for the student to have a study buddy available in each subject area.

When You See This Behavior	Try This Accommodation
8. Difficulty with any task that requires memory	Combine seeing, saying, writing, and doing; student may need to subvocalize to remember. Teach memory techniques as a study strategy (e.g., mnemonics, visualization, oral rehearsal, numerous repetitions).
9. Difficulty with test taking	Allow extra time for testing; teach test-taking skills and strategies and allow student to be tested orally. Use clear, readable, and uncluttered test forms. Use test format that the student is most comfortable with. Allow sample spaces for student response. Consider having lined answer spaces for essay or short-answer tests.
10. Confusion from nonverbal cues (misreads body language, etc.)	Directly teach (tell the student) what nonverbal cues mean. Model and have student practice reading cues in a safe setting.
11. Confusion from written material, difficulty finding the main idea of a paragraph, attributing greater importance to minor details	Provide student with a copy of reading material with main ideas underlined or highlighted. Provide an outline of important points from reading material. Teach outlining and main idea/details concepts. Provide tape of text/chapter.
12. Confusion from spoken material, lectures, and audiovisual material; difficulty finding main ideas from presentation; attributing greater importance to minor details	Provide student with a copy of presentation notes. Allow peers to share notes from presentation. Have student compare own notes with copy of peer's notes. Provide framed outlines of presentations, introducing visual and auditory cues to important information.
*13. Difficulty sustaining attention to tasks or other activities; easily distracted by extraneous stimuli	Reward attention. Break activities into small units. Reward timely accomplishments. Use physical proximity and touch. Use earphones or study carrels, quiet place, or preferential seating.
*14. Frequent messiness or sloppiness	Teach organizational skills. Be sure student has daily, weekly, or monthly assignment sheets, list of materials needed daily, and consistent format for papers. Have a consistent way for students to turn in and receive papers; reduce distractions. Give reward points for notebook checks and proper paper format. Provide clear copies of worksheets and handouts and consistent format for worksheets. Establish a daily routine; provide models for what you want the students to do. Arrange for a peer who will help with organization. Assist student to keep materials in a specific place (e.g., pencils in pouch). Be willing to repeat expectations.
15. Poor handwriting (often mixing: cursive with manuscript, and capitals with lowercase letters)	Allow for a scribe and grade for content, not handwriting. Allow for use of a computer or typewriter. Consider alternative methods for student responses (e.g., tape recorder, oral reports). Don't penalize student for mixing cursive and manuscript. Accept any method of production.
16. Difficulty with fluency in handwriting (e.g., good letter/word production but very slow and laborious)	Allow for shorter assignments (quality vs. quantity). Allow alternate method of production, such as computer, scribe, oral presentation, and so on.
17. Poorly developed study skills	Teach study skills specific to the subject area's organization (e.g., assignment calendar), textbook reading, note taking, finding main ideas/details, mapping, outlining, skimming, and summarizing.

When You See This Behavior	*Try This Accommodation*
18. Poor self-monitoring (e.g., careless errors in arithmetic, spelling, reading)	Teach specific methods of self-monitoring, e.g., "stop-look-listen." Have student proofread finished work after a day or two.
19. Low fluency or production of written material (takes hours on a ten-minute assignment)	Allow for alternative method for completing assignment (oral presentation, taped report, visual presentation, graphs, maps, pictures, etc., with reduced written requirements). Allow for alternative method of writing (e.g., typewriter, computer, cursive or printing, or a scribe).
*20. Apparent inattention (daydreaming, not here)	Get student's attention before giving directions. Tell the student how to pay attention: "Look at me when I talk"; "Watch my eyes when I speak." Ask student to repeat directions. Attempt to actively involve student in lesson (e.g., cooperative learning).
*21. Difficulty participating in class without being interruptive; difficulty working quietly	Seat student in close proximity to the teacher. Reward appropriate behavior; catch student "being good." Use study carrel if appropriate.
22. Inappropriate seeking of attention; clowns around; exhibits loud, excessive, or exaggerated movements as attention-seeking behavior; interrupts; butts into other children's activities; needles others	Show student (model) how to gain others' attention appropriately. Catch the student when appropriate and reinforce.
*23. Frequent, excessive talking	Teach student hand signals and use to tell student when and when not to talk. Make sure student is called when it is appropriate and reinforce listening.
24. Difficulty making transitions (from activity to activity or class to class), takes an excessive amount of time to find pencil, gives up, refuses to leave previous task, appears agitated during change	Program child for transitions. Give advance warning when a transition is going to occur. "Now we are completing the worksheet; next we will. . . ." Give the expectations for the transition: "and you will need. . . ." Specifically assemble and display lists of materials needed until a routine is possible. List steps necessary to complete each assignment. Have specific locations for all materials (e.g., pencil pouches, tabs in notebooks). Arrange for an organized helper (peer).
25. Difficulty remaining seated or in a particular position when required to	Give student frequent opportunities to get up and move around. Allow space for movement.
26. Frequent fidgeting with hands, feet, or objects; squirming in seat	Break tasks down into small increments and give frequent positive reinforcement for accomplishments (this type of behavior is often due to frustration). Allow alternative movement when possible.
27. Inappropriate responses in class often blurted out; answers given to questions before they have been completed	Seat student in close proximity to teacher so that visual and physical monitoring of student behavior can be done by the teacher. State behavior that you want. Tell the student how you expect him or her to behave.
28. Agitation under pressure and competition (academic or athletic)	Stress effort and enjoyment for self, rather than competition with others. Minimize timed activities; structure class for team effort and cooperation.

When You See This Behavior	Try This Accommodation
29. Inappropriate behaviors in a team or large-group sport or athletic activity; difficulty waiting for turn in games or group situations	Give the student a responsible job (e.g., class captain, care and distributing of the balls, score keeping); consider leadership role. Have the student in close proximity to teacher.
30. Frequent involvement with physically dangerous activities without considering possible consequences	Anticipate dangerous situations and plan for in advance. Stress stop, look, and listen. Pair with responsible peer. Rotate responsible students, so they don't wear out.
31. Poor adult interactions; defies authority	Provide positive attention. Talk with student about the inappropriate behavior. "What you are doing is. . . ." Suggest alternative method, "A better way of getting what you want is. . . ."
32. Frequent self-putdowns, poor personal care and posture, negative comments about self and others, poor self-esteem	Structure for success. Train student for self-monitoring, reinforce improvements, teach self-questioning strategies. (What am I doing? How is that going to effect others?) Allow opportunities for the student to show strengths. Give positive recognition.
33. Difficulty using unstructured time in special places such as recess, hallways, lunchroom, locker room, library, assembly	Provide student with a definite purpose during unstructured activities. "The purpose of going to the library is to check out books, etc. . . ." Encourage group games and participation (e.g., organized school clubs and activities).
*34. Losing things necessary for task or activities at school or at home (e.g., pencils, books; assignments before, during, and after completion of a given task)	Help student organize. Frequently monitor notebook and dividers, pencil, pouch, locker, book bag, desks. Provide positive reinforcement for good organization. Provide student with a list of needed materials and their locations.
35. Poor use of time (e.g., sitting, staring off into space, doodling, not working on task at hand)	Teach reminder cues (e.g., a gentle touch on the shoulder, hand signals). Tell the student your expectations of what paying attention looks like. "You look like you are paying attention when. . . ." Give the student a time limit for a small unit of work with positive reinforcement for accurate completion. Use of contract, timer, and so on, for self-monitoring.

SOURCE: Reprinted with permission from the California Association of School Psychologists. Copyright 1991. A version of this article can be found in the Winter 1998 edition of the GRADDA Newsletter.

NOTE: * Most dominant behaviors displayed by students with attention-deficit disorders.

Resource 18
American
Education Week Memo

MEMORANDUM

TO: All Faculty
FROM: Principal
DATE: November
RE: American Education Week

American Education week gives me another opportunity to thank you for the hard work and dedication that you demonstrate each and every day on behalf of the students and families of this school.

Working with students in an educational setting is a noble and honorable endeavor. Our daily interactions leave impressions and make a difference in the lives of the children of this school. They are the beneficiaries of our collective expertise, caring attitude, enthusiasm, and support. Your efforts and impact will be long lasting.

I know that you continually meet the challenge of creating a positive, student-centered learning environment in the classroom, the hallways, and throughout the school building and grounds. Please accept this small token of my appreciation for your significant contribution to the lives of our students.

As you walk from your car through the doors of this school, I hope you feel proud knowing that you are part of a team of professionals focused on meeting the needs of all students.

The upcoming Thanksgiving holiday will soon be upon us. Please enjoy the long weekend vacation knowing that this is a well-deserved rest and break from our school routines.

Resource 19
Fundraising Considerations

1. Select the item to sell. Know your dealer and the product before you commit to a sale. Check with other schools in your area and ask for references.

2. Will the company help with the sale, such as putting on a fundraising assembly?

3. Does the company furnish sales aids and sales charts, and do they have a prize and reward system? What sales incentive programs have worked at other schools that have sold their product(s)?

4. Will the company reserve your area for your sale only and not let other groups sell in the same area at the same time?

5. How much profit will you make on the item being sold?

6. Can unsold items be returned for a refund?

7. Can items that are not sold be sold later, or are they useless after a certain date?

8. Are the items in stock so that you can have quick delivery, or is it a special item that takes weeks for delivery?

9. Do the students sell the item, or do they take orders from sales kits, samples, or catalogs? (*Note:* Make sure that if they are selling from a catalog, there are no items that might be offensive, such as posters that disparage education or homework.)

10. What is your first impression of the sale item? Will it sell well at school or in the community? Make sure you get a broad sampling of students if it is something you want to sell on campus. How does it look, taste, smell, or work? Will the purchaser want or need it? Select an item the customer will really want and can use. Is the product a one-time sale, or will there be a chance for repeat sales? Is the price right for quick sales? Does the item have a proven sales record in similar communities?

SOURCE: Adapted from Laird, J. (1995). *Survival guide.* Reston, VA: National Association of Secondary School Principals.

Resource 20
Principal's Newsletter to Parents

November is upon us, and the upcoming Thanksgiving Day holiday will soon be celebrated. This traditional holiday celebration stirs happy thoughts, feelings, and fond memories for many. It is this sense of tradition that will serve as my theme for this edition of the Middle School PTA Newsletter and my principal's message.

Traditions help give us a sense of family and community and promote a feeling of belonging. Traditions help create pride and a history. The Thanksgiving Day holiday is a celebration that all families can enjoy. It is a time to get together and appreciate the company of one another. It also gives us the chance to be thankful for all that is positive in our lives: family, friends, health, and happiness.

This time of year gives me an opportunity to mention some of the other activities (traditions) that take place at our school—with the help of members of the Site-Based Management Team, our faculty and staff, and the PTA—such as yearbook, the school newspaper, sports teams, exchange programs, the eighth-grade graduation dance, monthly dances, winter and spring musical concerts, the art show, Honor Society induction, student government, and the many other after-school activities.

We are also working to create more events that will facilitate traditions within our school. We hope such activities and events will become yearly experiences to help establish the middle school as a center and focal point for families to share and celebrate success and learning.

During this upcoming November/December holiday season, let me promote a tradition through this newsletter message. I look forward to the many chances to personally wish you greetings at our upcoming events. Remember, in this upcoming season of gift giving, you are the gift!

Resource 21
Holiday Gifts:
A Challenge or a Burden

As we approach each holiday season, most of us feel a degree of pressure when we shop for our friends and loved ones. It's so easy to submit to the Madison Avenue hype or to the more covert persuasions of advertising campaigns. With time being precious, there is a tendency to quickly accomplish the task rather than to view our gift as being special and potentially quite meaningful.

Gift giving is probably the most wasted opportunity to expand either a child's educational horizons or to create and nurture a lifelong interest. When I speak with adults and reminisce about the impact of gifts they have received, some beautiful images emerge. Those who benefited from a friend or relative who took time to make an intelligent choice brighten and take pleasure in relating the ripple effects on their lives. Vistas were expanded, doors were opened, and successes were traced back to that one particular holiday.

A few days ago, I visited with a relative who had finished her holiday shopping far in advance of the important date. As she wrapped the gifts, it was clear to me that lots of money and little thought went into her purchases. Large cartons of plastic toys predominated, and even the stocking stuffers were akin to those one would find in a grammar school grab bag. I know my cousin was stunned and somewhat offended when I answered in the negative when she asked, "Aren't these kids lucky to get all these presents?"

After recovering from her initial hurt, we sat down and made a list of some better inexpensive gifts. Modeling clay replaced a water gun, drawing by numbers took the place of a slingshot, and we decided that some high-interest low-vocabulary books were to be placed under her child's pillow the night after the holiday. Some of the other articles were saved for other occasions, but many were exchanged to fund the new purchases. My cousin then went to work on her major purchases, not with disappointment but with newfound pride and confidence.

Her imagination and creativity went far beyond my expectations. Together with her friends we developed a group of suggestions, which we believe could help a child to learn something new or to build a more lasting interest in the future. They are not divided by age groups since that should be obvious to any adult. I also reject any socioeconomic argument about family wealth, since there are free and inexpensive gifts discussed as well.

This is truly the season of joy and peace. It is a time in which we express these emotions by our traditional exchange of presents. Your purchase is also a rare opportunity to affect someone's life. I hope you meet the challenge and are remembered for the meaningfulness of your gift.

A library card could open the world to any child. A weekly or bimonthly family library night would be a gift of family togetherness and probably better school grades.

A book is, in my opinion, a required present. Whenever your child wants to stay up late to read in bed, I'd not only recommend a positive response, but I'd try to motivate it. Did you ever see the marvelous selections of $.05 to $.25 books at garage sales?

A personal diary: People who write well do so because they write frequently. What a great way to motivate penmanship practice, creativity, and an ability to document one's own joys and traumas!

Collecting stamps or other items: While I was traveling out west one summer, a U.S. park ranger told me his interest in geology was awakened because an aunt gave him a small rock and mineral collection. Whether it be stamps, coins, or baseball cards, the child will learn history and develop personal expertise in a satisfying and creative way.

Examine the potential learning involved in a stamp or coin collection:

- Sequencing by dates
- Improved organization
- Increased historical knowledge
- Economics of supply and demand, since the coins and stamps that are most expensive are so because fewer were produced
- The appreciation for physically caring for one's possessions, since here too value is increased by the condition of the item

What an incredible number of lessons are understood when your children are their own teachers. They might even develop an appreciation for why you ask them to take care of their possessions!

Just as a worthwhile gift accomplishes the objective of stimulating additional learning, it also helps us to plan better presents for future occasions. If stamp collecting becomes an interest, it's logical that new albums, catalogs, journals, supplies, and equipment will be appreciated for the child's birthday and other happy events. Common sense can be contagious.

A subscription to a magazine is a great idea. Just listen to the names and your own imagination will project the possibilities for your child:

- *Science Digest*
- *Click*
- *Popular Mechanics*
- *Sesame Street*
- *National Geographic*
- *Ladybug*
- *Highlight*
- *Muse*
- *Cricket*
- *Spider*
- *Sports Illustrated for Kids*
- *Computer & Electronics*
- *Omni*

These are also gifts that continue to enrich their lives throughout the year. Any of the popular word games are appropriate since they help to reinforce the education the children are receiving in school. The young people who are playing Scrabble are much better off than those who contribute to the incredible statistic that the average child watches more hours of television by the time he or she enters school than a doctoral student spends in the classroom to earn a degree.

For our more affluent families, I hope that if you have purchased a computer game, you simply don't purchase every available game cartridge. In fact, I'd probably buy one educational tape and, as part of the gift, allow the child to buy one video game. Until the child makes the fun purchase sometime after the holiday, he or she will use his new machine with a learning tape. That's shrewd planning! Consider, also, the following gifts:

- A microscope
- Science kits that detail how the body functions or teach electrical concepts
- Chemistry sets
- Question-and-answer games
- Arithmetic puzzles or flash cards
- Map, compass, and telescope
- A basic tool set
- Knitting, crocheting, needlepoint, and rug-weaving supplies
- Crossword puzzles

Grandparents, aunts, and uncles have a similar opportunity. A friend with an interest in ballet said she thanks her aunt for making her aware of the arts. Her annual gift in good times was theater, ballet, and concert tickets. During their poverty era, it was the museums, the botanical gardens, and the zoo. Ultimately, it is not a matter of dollars and cents but rather the use of good sense.

Resource 22
Administrator's
Observation Worksheet

Teacher: _____   Date of Observation: _____ Period: _____

Subject: _____   Department: _____ Room: _____

Type of Class: H — R — NR — PSEN — Sp. Ed.   Number of Students: _____ Grade Level: _____

Try to describe the lesson as accurately and as objectively as you can. List what you see and hear, and avoid writing what you feel. If you feel something, then try to observe something to substantiate your feelings.

1. Learning Environment

a. *General appearance of the room:* Is it clean and attractively decorated? Does it promote a feeling of organization? _____

b. *Lighting:* Can students see their work clearly? _____

c. *Arrangement of the desks:* How are the desks arranged? Rows, clusters, horseshoe, etc.? _____

d. *Location of the teacher:* Where is the teacher in the classroom? Front, middle, back, mobile? _____
_____

e. *Location of the students:* Where were the students positioned? Front, middle, back, scattered?
_____

2. Student Involvement

a. *General attentiveness:* Were students paying attention? yes no Taking notes? yes no Following directions? yes no Asking questions? yes no

b. *General preparedness:* Did students have the necessary classroom tools: pen, pencils, paper, notebooks, textbooks? _____

c. *Rapport:* Did students actively get involved in the lesson? _____
Did they ask questions or answer questions? _____

3. Teacher Traits

a. *General appearance:* _____

b. *Body language:* Animated or dull? Friendly or threatening? _____

230

c. *Facial expressions:* Did the teacher's facial expressions convey feelings of warmth, understanding, hope, or excitement? _____

d. *Voice:* Tonal quality, diction, volume: monotonous or variable? negative or positive? harsh or calm? slow or fast? _____

e. Did the teacher use his or her voice to emphasize concepts? _____

f. Did the teacher use words of praise or respect for the students? _____

g. Did the teacher favor one side of the room or certain students? _____

h. Did the teacher achieve and maintain eye contact with the students? _____

i. Did the personality of the teacher come through in the lesson? _____

j. Did the teacher blend the subject matter with a warm, caring appreciation of the class? _____

k. Did the teacher express a sense of humor when appropriate? _____

l. Did the teacher smile? _____

4. Development of the Lesson

a. Was time allotted to review the previous night's homework assignment? _____

b. Was time allotted for a brief review of the previous lesson? _____

c. Was time allotted for an introduction for the lesson? _____

d. Was the lesson's objective clearly stated? _____

e. What method of presentation was used (e.g., lecture, discovery, Socratic, discussion)? _____ _____

f. Was the presentation method(s) appropriate? _____ Was it exciting, interesting, creative, and, most of all, successful? _____

g. Did the method invoke student participation? _____

h. Was appropriate language used in the presentation? _____

i. Were important definitions explained and written on the board? _____

j. Did the teacher outline or paraphrase important procedures or concepts during the lesson? _____

k. Were examples or practice problems given to illustrate and assess the students' understanding of the material? _____

l. Were diagrams, charts, or other learning aids used to illustrate key ideas? _____

5. Use of Materials

a. Was work on the board done neatly and in an organized manner? _____ Were diagrams highlighted with colored chalk? _____

b. Did the teacher point to the board to focus the class's attention on a specific point? _____ _____

c. Were prepared dittos used properly? _____ Were the dittos appropriate? _____

d. Were textbooks used? _____

e. Was an overhead projector, slides, or filmstrips used? _____

6. Questioning Techniques

Students' Questions and the Teacher's Response

a. Did the teacher use questions from students as opportunities for discussion? _____

b. Did the teacher capitalize on the questions that were asked? _____

c. Did the teacher use questions to lead into appropriate discussions? _____

d. Did the teacher encourage or discourage questions from the class? _____

e. How did the teacher react when questions were asked? With empathy, or was the student put down? _____

f. Did the teacher respond in an appropriate manner and with patience? _____

g. Did the teacher maintain the focus of the lesson without getting sidetracked? _____

h. Where did the questions come from? Were they scattered or coming from one or two individuals? _____

i. Did the teacher write important questions on the board? _____

j. How many student questions were asked? _____

Teacher-Generated Questions

a. Did the teacher use questions to lead into the lesson? _____

b. Did the teacher ask quality questions? _____

c. Were the questions vague or pointed? _____

d. Were the questions informational, open-ended, or rhetorical? _____

e. Did the teacher provide the student with sufficient time to answer the question? _____

f. How many questions did the teacher ask? _____

7. Teacher Motivation

a. Did the teacher get into the spirit of the lesson or merely go through the motions? _____

b. Did the teacher have a twinkle in his or her eye? Was the teacher dynamic? Enthusiastic? _____

c. Was the lesson interesting as well as informative? _____

8. Time Allocation of the Overall Lesson

a. Was the lesson balanced or overweighed in any way? _____

b. What was the overall pace (lethargic, slow, average, fast, too fast)? _____

c. Did the teacher change from one topic to another smoothly or abruptly? _____

d. When activities changed, was the change coordinated or disjointed? _____

9. Discipline

a. How did the teacher handle discipline problems or disruptions? _____

10. End of Lesson

a. Did the teacher summarize the lesson's major points? _____
b. Did the teacher assign homework? _____
c. Did the teacher allow time for concluding questions? _____
d. Did the teacher tie in the day's lesson with the overall unit? _____

11. Overall Reaction

a. Did the teacher conduct an organized, purposeful lesson? _____
b. Were the teacher's explanations clear, concise, detailed, and understood? _____
c. Did the teacher paraphrase the major points of the lesson? _____
d. Did the teacher reinforce the major points of the lesson? _____
e. Were in-class problems used to assess student comprehension? _____
f. Were the objectives of the lesson accomplished? _____

12. Overall Evaluation

Excellent   Very Good   Good   Fair   Unsatisfactory

13. Suggestions for Improvement

_____

_____

_____

_____

_____

_____

Resource 23
Rating Scale for
Custodial Services

School: _____ Date: _____

Signature of Evaluator: _____
Position of Evaluator: _____

To the Evaluator:
After careful study, assign a rating that best represents your judgment of the custodial service rendered in each area listed.

Rating key: Unsatisfactory (below standard)
               Satisfactory (up to minimum standard)
               Good (above average)
               Superior (outstanding, exceptional, very efficient)

Areas to inspect and rate include the following:

  1. _____ Boiler Room and Basement

  2. _____ Lavatories

  3. _____ Classrooms

  4. _____ Hallways

  5. _____ Stairways

  6. _____ Entrances

  7. _____ Auditorium

  8. _____ All-Purpose Rooms and Gymnasium

  9. _____ Cafeteria or Lunchroom

  10. _____ Shower Rooms

  11. _____ Locker Rooms

  12. _____ Teachers'/Faculty Rooms

  13. _____ Janitor Closets

  14. _____ Outside Grounds

15. _____ Motors

16. _____ Minor Repairs

17. _____ Custodial Personnel: Appearance and Personal Habits

18. _____ Reports and Records

Resource 24
Scheduling Timeline

Each school develops a timeline for scheduling activities based on local needs. The following example includes items that such a schedule might include.

Jan 10   Obtain estimated student enrollment.

Jan 15   Consult with elementary principals regarding student orientation/course selection process.

Jan 30   Meet with staff to develop and review course selection materials and orientation activities.

Feb 5   Prepare course selection materials; gather data regarding students (e.g., achievement, special services).

Feb 15   Meet with high school staff to develop transition activities.

Feb 20   Conduct parent orientation meetings.

Mar 1   High school counselors visit and conduct student orientation meetings.

Mar 15   Return ninth-grade materials to high school.

Mar 20   Deadline for sixth-, seventh-, and eighth-grade course selection sheets. Counselors edit, update, and correct them; secretaries enter into data system.

Mar 30   Materials sent to data processing.

Apr 1   High school counselors visit to review materials.

Apr 5   Course tallies available from data processing.

Apr 15   Staffing levels determined.

May 1   Preliminary master schedule developed.

May 10   Edit master schedule; conduct scheduling simulations.

May 20   Fifth graders visit.

Jun 1   Counselors resolve scheduling conflicts.

Jun 20   Receive preliminary class lists and schedules; finalize schedule on data system.

Aug 15   Adjust schedule based on summer changes; schedule newly enrolled students; request lists and schedules.

SOURCE: Adapted from Williamson, R. (1993). *Scheduling the middle level school to meet early adolescent needs.* Reston, VA: National Association of Secondary School Principals.

Resource 25
Inspirational Memorandum

Principal's Message—February

It's halftime, and as athletes meet with their coaches to discuss game performance and strategy for the second half, students need to meet with their families, counselors, and teachers to redirect, refocus, and review strategies, so they can be even more successful during the second half of the school year.

As the second half of the school year begins, let's take the time to remind ourselves to keep our kids focused by helping them manage their time to read every day, complete their assignments, and arrive at school on time and prepared for the day's work ahead. These activities and responsibilities are essential to a successful academic school year. The academic school year remaining requires us to inspire our students to complete the good work achieved these past months and finish the school year with the same determination. Now is also the time for students who have not developed positive work habits and academic success to do so.

To date, this has been a terrific school year. Let's finish our work together so that our students will continue to develop good work habits and maintain positive attitudes that will enable them to meet the educational challenges that we place before them.

In addition, many fabulous events are being planned for the second half of the school year. You will be receiving announcements, updates, and reminders. Hopefully, you will be able to attend and participate.

On behalf of the faculty and staff at the middle school, we look forward to your continued cooperation and support.

Sincerely,

Your Middle School Principal

Resource 26
Interview Questions for Teachers

1. Welcome, Ms./Mr. [*Candidate's Name*]. Please tell us something about yourself.

2. Other than your most recent student teaching experience, what experience(s) have you had working with children?

3. What special talents might you bring into your classroom?

4. Could you please tell us what your preparation to teaching has entailed?

5. What might your classroom look like?

6. Please take a few moments to prepare for us a letter you might wish to send to your students in August, prior to the start of the upcoming school year.

7. How might you address the child who is disruptive in class?

8. How would appropriate classroom behavior be made known to students?

9. What do you consider to be the most important aspect of teaching?

10. What was the last book you read? Tell us something about it. (*If interviewers are familiar with the book cited, be prepared for some banter about the book.*)

11. If a child in your class were experiencing difficulties, what recourse might you commence?

12. What do you perceive as your strengths? Your weaknesses?

13. How might you address the needs of a very quiet, unassuming, nonparticipating child? An extremely vocal, excitable child?

14. Now that you have recently graduated, how might you continue to enhance your professional knowledge and skills?

15. To which professional organizations do you belong?

Resource 27
Sample Letter Sent to All Those Running for School Offices

October

Re: Student Council Elections

Dear (*Student's Name*),

Many thanks for your participation in running for elected office during the recent student government election process at school.

I appreciate all of the hard work that it took for you to place yourself in nomination for an elected office. After asking students and teachers to sign your petition, you created campaign posters and wrote and recorded your election speech.

Your courage to seek elected office makes me very proud of you. Walking in the halls and seeing your campaign posters helps me remember that your willingness to participate in this process teaches everyone in school about the importance of voting and electing people to leadership positions.

It is unfortunate that every candidate cannot be elected, but every candidate is a winner! You have shown us your leadership potential, and I encourage you to continue to strive to be the best that you can be. I know your family is proud of your accomplishments at school. We are proud of you and want you to know you have earned the respect of your classmates, teachers, and principal.

On behalf of everyone in school, thank you for your involvement. It helps everyone value the election process. Without you, we would not have a strong student government.

Sincerely,

Your Middle School Principal

Resource 28
Rating Your
Middle School Principal

Instructions: Circle your rating of your principal's performance for each of the following listed skills. Use the rating scale below.

Rating scale: 1 = Exceeds district expectations
                 2 = Meets district expectations
                 3 = Needs improvement

Major Duties as Specified in Job Description

Develops and supervises the total instructional program
1   2   3

Demonstrates skill in hiring new staff members and works with all staff to ensure maximum opportunity for success
1   2   3

Effectively develops and manages the budget as assigned to the building
1   2   3

Advocates school improvement/reform and encourages staff to be innovative in the delivery of education; leads productive faculty meetings to ensure that lines of communication are open
1   2   3

Is an effective evaluator of instruction and able to make objective decisions regarding the retention or dismissal of personnel
1   2   3

Effectively manages an efficient office and record-keeping system
1   2   3

Demonstrates care and concern for the well-being of all students and staff
1   2   3

Develops a fair and consistent system for student discipline
1   2   3

Effectively develops and administers an objective system for the evaluation of all classified staff
1   2   3

Establishes positive public relations within and outside the school; encourages staff to do the same
1   2   3

Maintains professional knowledge through attendance at selected conferences, readings of professional journals, or memberships in professional organizations
1   2   3

Is successful in developing and achieving annual personal and professional goals
1   2   3

Personal and Professional Qualities

Defends principle and conviction in the face of pressure and partisan influence
1   2   3

Maintains high personal and professional standards of ethics, honesty, and integrity
1   2   3

Earns respect and standing among professional colleagues
1   2   3

Devotes time and energy effectively to the position
1   2   3

Is a team player and contributor
1   2   3

Exercises good judgment and the democratic process in arriving at decisions
1   2   3

Possesses and maintains the health and energy necessary to meet the responsibilities of the position
1   2   3

Is professionally attired and well-groomed
1   2   3

Demonstrates effective command of language (written and oral) in dealing with staff, board members, and the public
1   2   3

Speaks well in front of large and small groups; expresses ideas in a logical and forthright manner
1   2   3

Maintains professional development through reading, coursework, conference attendance, professional committee work, visits to other schools, and meetings with other administrators
1   2   3

Demonstrates loyalty to the organization and to colleagues
1   2   3

Is progressive in his or her thinking and effectively plans for organizational improvement
1   2   3

Is a positive emissary for the district within the community
1   2   3

Resource 29
Teacher's Comments for Interim Reports and Report Cards

For Interim Reports Only (you must choose one from this first group for each student)

1. Currently failing

2. Currently passing but near failing

3. Currently passing but needs improvement

4. Currently passing

5. Currently passing and doing well

6. Student just entered the class

Complimentary Comments

7. Excellent academic achievement

8. Good effort, trying hard

9. Improvement shown

10. Good speaking skills

Corrective Comments

11. Incomplete: make up within five weeks

12. Decline in effort/grade

13. Inconsistent effort

14. Poor test/quiz grades

15. Homework/class work missing or incomplete

16. Fundamental skills are weak

17. Absences/lateness affects grade

18. Has not made up missed work

19. Must speak/participate more

20. Speaking skills weak

21. Poor listening comprehension

22. Has difficulty writing essays

23. Research project not completed

24. Missed labs affect grade

25. Lab reports missing or poor

Attendance Comments

26. No mark: many legal absences

Recommendations

27. Attitude in class needs improvement

28. More study/practice needed

29. Recommend extra help

30. Please call for conference

Behavior/Attitude

31. Positive contributor to class

32. Shows exceptional interest

33. Behavior has improved

34. Courteous and cooperative

35. Numerous absences

36. Frequently late to class

37. Often unprepared for class

38. Behavior not acceptable

Comments by Department

Art Education

39. Excellent artworks

40. Artworks satisfactory

41. Improvement demonstrated in artworks

42. Needs improvement in the quality of artworks

43. Incomplete artworks

Business Education

44. Did not complete class assignments

45. Respectful use of equipment

46. Refuses to do work

47. Has stopped attending class

48. Continues to hand in assignments late

English/Language Arts

49. Written work needs improvement

50. Oral skills need improvement

51. Vocabulary needs to be expanded

52. Book reports were not completed

53. Handwriting needs improvement

Foreign Language Education

54. More classroom participation needed

55. Behavior is inconsistent

56. Not working to ability

57. Frequently interrupts instruction

58. Quality of written work needs improvement

Health Education

59. Class cutting is affecting grade negatively

60. Difficulty cooperating in group activities

61. Unable to focus on task

62. Vigorous, enthusiastic, and excited about learning

63. Continually contributes to the dialog of the class

Mathematics Education

64. Computer programming assignments missing/unsatisfactory

65. Completion rates of units must improve

66. Notebook is disorganized/unsatisfactory or missing

67. Inappropriate use of time in class

68. Take-home assignments/exams not submitted

Music/Performing Arts Education

69. Excellent performance

70. Competent performance

71. Needs improvement in performance skills

72. Poor lesson attendance

73. Missed required concert/performance

Physical Education

74. Nearing maximum number of absences/unprepareds

75. Failed to submit PE notebook or notebook incomplete

76. Failure to follow directions and uncooperative

77. Sportsfolio work missing

78. Needs to make up missing test(s)

Science Education

79. Lab reports not submitted

80. Lab reports are unsatisfactory

81. In danger of not meeting the Regent's lab requirements

82. Exceptional lab effort

83. Poor comprehension of science vocabulary

Social Studies Education

84. Required research not completed

85. Reading comprehension needs improvement

86. Projects incomplete/unsatisfactory

87. Oral/written presentation not completed

88. Outstanding course participation

Special Education

89. Organizational skills need improvement

90. Failing tests

91. Note taking needs improvement

92. Needs to pay closer attention

93. Working cooperatively with others

Technology Education

94. Final project not completed

95. Respectful use of equipment

96. Refuses to do work

97. Frequently requires special attention

98. Poor language skills impede learning

Resource 30
Student Activities
Evaluation Report

TO: Advisor's Name
FROM: Administrator's Name
DATE: Today's Date
RE: Student Activity Advisor: End-of-Year Evaluation

Activity: Photography Club
Meetings: Regular—1 per week
Membership: Regular—16 Students
Major Events: Trips taken to special photographic places: Bronx Zoo, Museum of Art; Take pictures
at major school-related events, Art/Photo Show, Contests

Evaluation:

Outstanding	Satisfactory	Not Applicable	
X			Rapport With Students
	X		Frequency of Meetings
X			Supervision of Club Events
X			Supervision of Fundraising Activities
X			Supervision of Club's Financial Matters
	X		Club Bulletin Board Display
X			Timely Submission of Forms & Questionnaires
	X		Public Relations
X			Overall Performance

Summary:

The purpose of the Photography Club is to provide enrichment to students who wish to learn and
develop their photographic abilities and techniques. By sharing your expertise and enthusiasm, our
students learn photographic style and skill beyond what we have time to teach in our ordinary classes.
Your knowledge, expertise, and willingness to share your time are greatly appreciated.

Please accept my congratulations for another successful year.

_____   _____
Advisor's Signature   Student Activities Coordinator

Resource 31
Final Examination Schedule

<hr>

May 27

Dear Parents:

The following information details the end-of-the-year procedures for our middle school students.

Date	Time	Final Exam Subject	Bus Dismissal
Monday, June 17	12:30 P.M.–2:40 P.M.	Mathematics	2:55 P.M.
Tuesday, June 18	8:15 A.M.–10:15 A.M.	Science	10:30 A.M.
Wednesday, June 19	8:15 A.M.–10:15 A.M.	English	10:30 A.M.
Thursday, June 20	8:15 A.M.–10:15 A.M.	Social Studies	10:30 A.M.

School Lunch Services. The breakfast and lunch programs will operate daily through Friday, June 14.

Lost Books. Payment for lost or damaged textbooks and library books can be made through June 24 in the main office. All students are reminded of their responsibilities and obligations. Report cards may be held for those students who owe any monies or books.

Report Cards. Report cards will be mailed home after June 28.

Activity and Athletic Bus Runs. The last day for athletic buses (4:45 P.M.) is Thursday, June 13, and the last day for activity buses (3:45 P.M.) is Friday, June 14.

Summer Hours. Our middle school will be closed July 29 until August 12. Members of the administrative and clerical staff will be in attendance on all other days to assist you between the hours of 8:00 A.M. and 2:30 P.M. If you have any questions, please feel free to call the main office and leave your question on our answering machine.

Very truly yours,

Your Middle School Principal

Resource 32
Locker Cleanup

MEMORANDUM

TO: All Staff
FROM: Principal
DATE: June
RE: Locker Cleanup

The following outlines the procedures we will use to clean out all student lockers and to relock them for the summer months.

1. On the last day of school, we will conduct a schoolwide locker cleanup during Period 2. Garbage pails and bins will be placed in all hallways for students to discard items they no longer need.

2. Locker cleanup day will be announced to all students over the public address system and through an official notice, which will be distributed to all students prior to the actual cleanup date.

3. At the end of the school day, students will be requested to remove all items from their lockers, remove their locks from the lock's locking mechanism, and lock it to the handle just above the locking hole. This will allow our custodians to enter the locker to disinfect and make any physical adjustments that are needed.

4. Two office workers will then open any locks that are still in the locking hole and will remove all items from those lockers. They will place all valuables in a plastic bag and place the locker number and the student name on the bag for future reference.

5. Any textbooks or library books found in lockers will be returned to the appropriate departments or the library.

6. After the office workers have completed their final cleanup, the custodial staff will check each locker and make repairs as needed. Once this is accomplished, the office workers will relock (using the locking hole) all lockers, switch different locks onto the lockers of graduating eighth graders, and record these changes in the locker book.

We hope everything outlined here will go smoothly!

Please contact the main office if you have any questions. As always, thanks for your help.

To All Students

Locker Cleanup Day—Friday, June 12

Scheduled to take place on the last day of classes during homeroom. Please follow the procedures listed below:

- All students are asked to throw out any items that they no longer need.
- Garbage bins will be located in the hallways for your use.
- You may keep all other items in your locker till the end of the school day.
- At the end of the day, you must remove all items from your locker and remove the lock from the lock's locking hole and lock it on the handle just above the hole. This will keep your lock safe till next year and will give our custodial staff access to clean your locker and fix any mechanical parts that might not be working properly.
- Graduating eighth graders should follow the same procedure. Their locks will be collected by staff from the main office, and they will be credited for returning their locks if they lock them on the handle. Any graduating eighth grader who fails to lock the lock on the handle will be charged $4 to replace the lock issued at the beginning of the year.

Good luck on your finals!

Resource 33
End-of-Year Sign-Out List

Your Middle School

NOTE: Please write NA where an item is not applicable.   Teacher: _____

Item	Required Initials
Bulletin boards cleared and classroom prepared for the summer	_____ Dept. Coordinator
Final examinations: Rated–Arranged–Filed	_____ Principal's Secretary
All failure slips submitted	_____ Guidance Coordinator
Report card scan forms completed and submitted	_____ Guidance Coordinator
Report card verification forms completed and submitted	_____ Guidance Coordinator
Requisitions submitted	_____ Principal's Secretary
Book inventory submitted	_____ Principal's Secretary
Rebind list submitted	_____ Principal's Secretary
Science lab books/folders completed for science courses	_____ Science Secretary
Regents' report submitted (accelerated courses only)	_____ Principal's Secretary
Grade book submitted with teacher name on cover	_____ Principal's Secretary

Summer Address: _____

Summer Phone: _____

All keys labeled and returned (for retirees only)   _____
                                                       Head Custodian

Teacher manual returned to main office   _____
                                                       Principal's Secretary

Final check by principal   _____
                                                       Principal

References

Austin, Diane. (n.d.). *Characteristics of the middle school child.* Shreveport, LA: Author.

Bergmann, S. (1991). Guidance in the middle level school: The compassion component. In J. Capelluti & D. Stokes (Ed.), *Middle level education programs, policies, and practices* (pp. 48–53). Reston, VA: National Association of Secondary School Principals.

Haiman, F. (1951). *Group leadership and democratic action.* Boston: Houghton Mifflin.

Laird, J. (1995). *Survival guide.* Reston, VA: National Association of Secondary School Principals.

National Association of Secondary School Principals. (n.d.). *Schools in the middle* [Brochure]. Reston, VA: Author.

National Association of Secondary School Principals. (2002). Principals' legislative action center. *Bulletin, 86*(631). Retrieved March, 2003, from http://www.principals.org/news/bltn_ll_ml0602.html

New York State Education Department Blue Ribbon Panel on School Leadership. (2000). *Essential knowledge and skills for effective school leadership characteristics* [Report]. New York: Author.

Ricken, R. (1984). *Love me when I'm most unlovable: The middle school years.* Reston, VA: National Association of Secondary School Principals.

Washington State Special Education, Office of Superintendent of Public Instruction. (1994). *Attention deficit hyperactivity disorders handbook: Guidelines for educators, health care providers, and parents.* Retrieved May, 2003, from http://www.k12.wa.us/SpecialEd/Publications/ADHD_handbook.asp

Williamson, R. (1993). *Scheduling the middle level school to meet early adolescent needs.* Reston, VA: National Association of Secondary School Principals.

**CORWIN
PRESS**

The Corwin Press logo—a raven striding across an open book—represents the happy union of courage and learning. We are a professional-level publisher of books and journals for K-12 educators, and we are committed to creating and providing resources that embody these qualities. Corwin's motto is "Success for All Learners."